TOOLS
OF THE
WRITER'S CRAFT

Other works by Sands Hall

Catching Heaven, a novel

Fair Use, a drama

Little Women, a stage adaptation of
the novel by Louisa May Alcott

TOOLS OF THE WRITER'S CRAFT

SANDS HALL

Moving Finger Press

SAN FRANCISCO
WWW.MOVINGFINGERPRESS.COM

Tools
of the
Writer's Craft

SECOND EDITION   SEPTEMBER 2007
COPYRIGHT ©2005, 2007 SANDS HALL

PRINTED IN THE UNITED STATES OF AMERICA
ISBN 978-0-9727225-7-5   SAN 254-9972

THIS BOOK IS FOR
MARY BOLTON
WHO TAUGHT SO MUCH,
AND MADE US LAUGH, TOO.
1926-2004

CONTENTS

I. The Essays

II.   The Exercises

INTRODUCTION:
"ACCORDING TO ME"

During a trip to Oaxaca a few years ago, my family and I visited nearby Monte Alban, a pre-Columbian ruin scattered across the top of a low mountain. As we piled out of the van, we were approached by a number of tour guides, waving their arms, showing off their English, offering their services. My partner at the time, Tom, asked one of the most insistent, "Are you any good?" and Francisco replied, with a flourish, "I am the worst." And since in my family the language of irony is always beguiling, off we headed with Francisco. As we walked the grassy plain, stopping at pyramids, stone walls, ball courts, and peering at the many loose slabs the size and shape of dictionaries that tilted this way and that, and which bore weathered petroglyphs, Francisco regaled us with Monte Alban's history. It had been an international pre-Columbia hospital, and a port; when an ocean used to cover central Mexico (he told us), lapping at the very edges of the hill on which we were standing, vessels came from Greece, India, China, bearing gold and patients; this explained the petroglyphed slabs, which were, he lectured, records of medical anomalies. Monte Alban was where tennis was invented. With each of these plausible/preposterous stories he would point to himself and say, "According to me...."

These essays are offered in that spirit. They record where I am in my understanding of craft, which continues to change and alter and expand. As I say as every class of mine begins, I am one teacher, and in class or out, you will have many. Some of what you read here will be useful; some will go against what you have been taught or have figured out for yourself; some will be dismissed under the banner of "personal style"; some will make more sense when you hear it, perhaps hear it differently, from another teacher, mentor, or—often—a fellow writer.

I have repeated the phrase, "according to me," so often that a student, Randall Buechner, managed to capture the gesture that accompanies it.

In addition to being a writer, I am an actor and a director; I also sing and play the guitar and mandolin. As I moved away from the initial high attached to just doing these things, I became increasingly interested in the craft of them: How is it <u>done</u>? How do those who are effective <u>do it</u>? How does art get made?

Several times a week I work out in my living room, near a carved Chinese chest that was a gift from my mother; it belonged to her father. As I do ab work and stretches and standing balance pose I find myself admiring this chest: its intricately carved surface, its proportions, and particularly one of its corners, which is often in my sit-up view. It's a "dove-tailed" corner, a corner that (I've heard) is both precise and long-lasting. Peering at it often leads to thoughts about the beauty of tools and the craft to put them to use. It takes skill and understanding and practice to create such a chest, to build a desk, bind a book, throw a pot, write a novel: things of beauty and utility. While nothing can ultimately explain or replace genius—or timing— we can improve our craft, so as to be ready when genius may strike; at the very least be able to do what we intend to do effectively and with purpose. As an acquaintance at the Iowa Writers' Workshop once said, "You either get bored or you get better."

My father, Oakley Hall, is the author of over two dozen novels, a libretto, and two books on writing. He and my mother, photographer Barbara Hall, are among the co-founders of the Community of Writers at Squaw Valley; my sister Brett is its Executive Director; her husband, novelist Louis B. Jones, is one of the fiction directors. While I grew up in a literary household, and although I have scribbled in journals much of my life, writing was not an early vocation. To some degree I think that early on I was a puzzle to, if not the despair of, my parents: although they were always happy we were reading something, my bottomless and years-long passion for Georgette Heyer's Regency Romances might have been slightly galling. When I was thirteen, during an on-site interview at a private high school, I was asked to write an essay about a novel I had recently read; in the car heading home there were some expostulations when I revealed that my chosen subject was *Gone with the Wind*. Not that *Gone with the Wind* isn't a perfectly fine novel. But it's part of the genre known as the romance novel, and in the book-filled upbringing that was mine there was perhaps some expectation that my choice might have been more "literary": *David Copperfield, Catcher in the Rye, A Separate Peace*. (As the years have gone by I have come to realize that much successful so-called genre fiction employs many of the elements that literary fiction does—and that literary fiction can be considered a genre too.)

So, even though I don't think of writing as an early passion, there is a telling incident that occurred when I was about seventeen: I remember moaning on about wanting to be a writer, and my father asked, "Do you want to be a writer, Sands? Or do you want to write? There is a difference." I realized that perhaps I was looking at the persona of being, versus the experience of doing. For years, until I began to write steadily, and to publish, I was quiet about the matter.

THE ESSAYS

As a result of so many summers spent participating in the Community of Writers at Squaw Valley, I am fortunate to know many extraordinary authors. However, perhaps because of an early tangle with Shakespeare in my freshman year of high school, I headed in the direction of theatre, and a different literary form. A beloved teacher, Wells Kerr, had us memorize Act One, Scene One of *Macbeth*—"When shall we three meet again..."—and I was hooked; that affection only grew as encounters with Shakespeare's plays and poetry, and an understanding of his craft, mounted. I pursued theatre through a BA in Acting, training at San Francisco's American Conservatory Theatre, stints at various Shakespeare Festivals, four years in New York, and ten in Los Angeles. It was in Hollywood, in my late thirties—when most of the marrow had been sucked from my bones (among other things, I had become an actress with, gasp, wrinkles on her face)—that I applied to graduate school and was accepted by the Iowa Writers' Workshop. At the end of my two years there I began to teach, and it was in trying to articulate my thoughts about writing to those students that these essays began to form. They originally came about because I found that I was scribbling similar comments, again and again, in the margins of student and client manuscripts. The essays became a sort of shorthand, as in, "see my thoughts about this in the attached." Then I began to include them in course packs of various classes, as a way to ensure that everyone in a given class would share, if briefly, a sensibility and nomenclature. I was often told they were useful, perhaps because of the theatre analogies and acting terminology employed, and although the world probably does not need yet another writing book, yet here one is.

The "tools" included in this volume come in the form of these essays, and exercises. The exercises are guides, ways to implement the ideas, the tools, proposed in the essays—what is intended as a balance of theory and practical application. But other than that, in spite of the book's title, there is no overarching or linking metaphor. I don't discuss Show, Don't Tell as a screwdriver, Metaphor as a flashlight, or Point of View as a hammer—although in fact the essays do hammer on a bit about that particular issue. Still, as my own writing and my interests have changed over the years, so has my point of view on point of view, and on other craft issues as well, and will no doubt continue to change. As with everything in this volume, there is no absolute; the perspective is simply "according to me."

THE EXERCISES

A dancer does daily plies, a pianist scales; an actor rehearses. Art—craft—requires practice. In my efforts to

confront and solve issues of craft and other writing problems, I devise exercises for myself—practice pieces that as
often as not become something I can incorporate into a
larger piece—and a few years ago I began to include these
in my courses.

Several of these are suggested at the end of each essay, as a way for the reader to apply the tools he or she's
just read about—to put the theory into practice. Several of
the exercises are suggested numerous times; the focus
shifts with each application.

In addition to the writer who may utilize the exercises as a way to hone her craft or launch or deepen a story
on which she's working, the exercises may be useful to
writers who are meeting as a group and want a more specific focus on writing craft than prompts or free-writes—
useful though those are—might supply.

The book is not constructed as a "how-to," as in "do
these exercises in order and you will have a story." Nor is
the emphasis in this volume on "finding your story," or
"discovering your plot." What the exercises will help you do
is: Discover and/or deepen your characters, understand
what drives them, put them into revealing situations, get
them to talk to one another, and experiment with point of
view. In the process, you may well discover what drives
your plot and/or find the story you have been intending to
write.

Somewhere between the essays and the exercises
you will begin to own some tools that you can put to work,
an understanding of craft that you can manipulate to make
the Chinese chest of your novel or story effective, and precise and useful and beautiful as well.

To my many students, who taught and teach me so
much, this book is gratefully dedicated.

MAKING WORKSHOPS WORK

The workshop begins. Perhaps you've met an instructor and some of your workshop peers and have an idea of what the expectations are for the weekend, the week, the next semester.

Perhaps you've also been handed a number of manuscripts.

Now what do you do? What does the workshop—not to mention the author whose work is under examination—expect from you?

Writing workshops are today so ubiquitous that it's hard to believe they haven't always been in existence. But Charles Dickens and Flaubert did not sit around a table with a number of other writers discussing whether or not having Oliver lose *both* parents isn't melodramatic, or if Emma Bovary's death—that tongue and all—isn't just a *bit* over the top. Nor did Hemingway, Welty, or Austen have their manuscripts picked apart by a jury of their peers.

What each of these writers probably did have is at least one or perhaps a group of friends—or a trusted mentor—who read and critiqued their work. Some of the writers mentioned above sat at the knee of those who preceded them: Hemingway relied on the advice of Gertrude Stein and Ezra Pound, Faulkner on that of Sherwood Anderson. And of course certain editors, Maxwell Perkins for example, are legendary figures.

A postcard on the wall of my study, which has traveled with me and is perforated from having been tacked over the years above many a desk, reads:

> Sands:
>
> Here is Ezra Pound's advice to Ernest Hemingway:
>
> > Use no superfluous words.
> >
> > No adjective that does not reveal something.
> >
> > Go in fear of abstractions.
>
> Love,
>   O.

We know how thoroughly Hemingway took his mentor Mr. Pound's advice. And a mentor of mine passed that good advice along. These days, however, we seldom hear a writer referring to his mentor, or "master." Perhaps because the notion of "apprenticing" has fallen largely out of favor, perhaps because as a society we have come to rely on group processes and committee meetings, the desire for a consensus of opinion has become more common. Thus the workshop—a forum for critical thinking—has become a popular and widespread phenomenon.

While the pros and cons of the workshop "system" can be endlessly debated, you are probably reading this with the expectation that your manuscript is about to be given criticism by a group of your peers. It behooves us to find a way to make a workshop, and the criticism that takes place within it, a constructive experience.

In her biography of Jane Austen, *Letters to Alice*, author Fay Weldon writes that Jane's first audience was her family: she would read her rough drafts to them in the parlor and ask for their responses to the story and characters. Let us work with the idea that a workshop is simply a formalized version of Jane Austen's situation: we are friends (or even family); each of us brings some literary understanding to the table; we are gathered together to tell each other what is working and what is not in our fiction.

We must do this with a great deal of respect: for the work, and for the endeavor. When the workshop is over, you will return to your yellow pad, your typewriter, your computer screen, and continue to write. As a workshop participant, part of your task is to ensure that each of your peers returns to work excited by what they have discovered about their writing, eager to apply what they have learned. This will be accomplished through respect, and the earnest desire to help each writer improve his or her manuscript.

A writer may choose to join a writing workshop for inspiration—or to experience a sense of community, rare in our vocation. A workshop also offers a pragmatic opportunity to give and receive feedback on the art and craft of writing. The invigorating process of a workshop—these days of intense communion with our peers—can help sustain us through the sometimes lonely days, weeks, months the discipline of writing demands. How can the study of manuscripts, usually the focus of the workshop process, provide us with the education, the insight, and the inspiration we desire?

We may begin writing with the entire arc of a story clear in our minds but as we continue to write this clarity vanishes. Sometimes we have a terrific beginning, but then what? Sometimes we begin with an ending in mind and try to force our characters into actions that will fulfill this final image. However it happens, all too often, in the process of stringing sentences together, we grow frustrated—and our story, short or long, slips from our grasp.

In this regard workshops can be very helpful. They can help us recover the original germ of a story that has gotten lost; can assist with an ending that doesn't pull together; and, perhaps most valuable, can help us find the story we didn't know we were telling.

But above all, in the process of critiquing manuscript after manuscript, a workshop gives us insights: into art, craft, and technique.

It is important to remember that the manuscript is why you are in a workshop. This vital detail often gets lost, especially in a short week that may offer lectures and meetings and connections. Those sheets of paper—the ones you and your fellow writers have slaved over—become a secondary activity. If you are part of an ongoing writer's group, which meets several times a month, life itself manages to intervene. But in fact, you are in a workshop because of manuscripts. You are here to have yours discussed; you are here to read, critically, the manuscripts of others.

YOU ARE HERE TO READ, CRITICALLY, THE MANUSCRIPT

Let's take a look at this word, critical. In addition to the meaning that it is something essential to a given endeavor, the usual sense of the word *criticism*, or the phrase *to criticize*, is "to react to something negatively." But that's limited. Here are a few definitions, courtesy of Webster's, to consider anew:

> **critical:**   Marked by careful and exact judgment and evaluation.
>
> **criticism:**   The art, skill or profession of making discriminating judgments, especially of literary or artistic works.

Note: This does not say negative judgments, but, rather, careful and discriminating ones.

> **discriminating:** Capable of recognizing or making fine distinctions: perceptive.

Thus, a workshop gives a group of perceptive people the opportunity to make perceptive comments and discriminating judgments of literary work.

It is not a place to practice shredding, scalping, and ego-blasting. Nor is it a contest in being "nice." And if someone said nasty things about your manuscript yesterday, swallow your pride and your urge for revenge and attend to your work today, even if it means pointing out excellence in their work.

And here is this amazing thing: the more thoroughly you read the manuscripts of others, the better your own editorial eye will become. This critical—and I mean that in both senses of the word—ability is what you can take back to your own work.

I have read that the Sanskrit root of the verb *to judge* means *to separate the wheat from the chaff*. This might be a valuable resonance to keep in mind when your head is reeling at the end of a workshop.

And now to some pragmatics.

PREPARING A MANUSCRIPT FOR DISCUSSION IN WORKSHOP

When you first sit down with a story or a section of a novel, read it at least twice, the first time without a pencil in your hand or criticism in mind. Give it the same kind of attention you would a story in a literary magazine or a book a respected friend has lent you. For example, try not to leap to immediate and negative judgments about authorial idiosyncrasies; these just might turn out to represent a personal and distinctive writing style.

Then take a few moments to think about the effect the story or novel segment created. Give yourself time to do this job well. **This is what each of you has joined the workshop to receive: A detailed, thoughtful analysis of your manuscript.**

THINGS TO THINK ABOUT

CHARACTERS:

Do you care about them? Well-drawn characters aren't necessarily likable, but has the author succeeded in having you engage with them?

→   Are they fleshed out adequately?

→   Does the author succeed in making them unique? Or are they walking clichés?

→   Do their motivations make sense and drive them through the story?

→   Are they consistent in their actions and their dialogue? If not, do these inconsistencies tell you something about them, or about the plot?

PLOT:

→   What happens?

→   Does someone change?

→ Is the story or chapter intriguing; did the writer succeed in creating a sense of tension?

It might be helpful to keep in mind that plot is not only what happens, but also the order in which a reader *discovers* what happens.

Sometimes a simple summary of the plot can be helpful to the writer and may lead to other questions:

→ Does the story or chapter start before it needs to? End too long after the scene's climax?

→ Are scenes included that are not necessary?

POINT OF VIEW:

→ Is the piece written in First Person? Third Person? Changing or Rotating? Omniscient?

→ Is the point of view consistent? Are there changes in perspective that are jarring?

→ Does the point of view chosen to tell the story seem to be the most effective one possible?

→ Are vocabulary, grammar, even punctuation consistent with the character of the chosen point of view?

VOICE (RELATED TO BOTH POINT OF VIEW AND LANGUAGE):

→ Is the voice consistent or does it waver?

→ Did you find it intrusive, or is it right for the story being told?

LANGUAGE:

→ Is the author's language elegant? Realistic? Vivid, boring, cerebral? (Clearly, this contributes to the quality of the voice.)

→   Is the language true to the narrator, the point of view telling the story? Or is it the language of the author? (This may be a matter of "style"; not necessarily more or less effective, but it's good to note: either way, is it purposeful?)

→   Is the writer's use of language clichéd, or do interesting turns of phrase strike you with their unique "take" on the world?

→   Does the author use strong verbs?

→   Are figures of speech used unusually and well?

DETAIL:

→   Does the author use detail well?

→   Are the details intrinsic to the characters and story, or does their inclusion seem merely "writerly?"

→   Does a given detail advance character? And/or plot? And/or theme?

→   You might examine the writer's use of metaphor: do objects and incidents in the manuscript represent more than their "surface" meaning? Are these consistent with the thematic concerns of the story?

DIALOGUE:

→   Is it believable?

→   Is it appropriate to the characters and to the style of the story?

→   Does it help to round out the characters?

→ Is there a dependence on adverbs in the attributions (*he said, calmly; she commented, angrily* or—my favorite—*she asked, interrogatively*) to communicate tone? That is, does the author tell, or show how the characters are behaving?

→ Is there too little dialogue?

→ Is there too much: does the author depend on characters to literally tell the story?

→ Is dialogue-as-exposition handled deftly? Awkwardly?

CONTENT:

→ Is this a story you've read before?

→ Or does it give you a fresh look at the world, asking you to think about something in a new way?

→ Would you like to read more about this world, or by this author?

→ If the manuscript is a chapter in a novel, would you want to read on?

THEME:

→ Note: Some authors maintain that they are not interested in theme, or that if there is one, it is not "purposeful": this is disingenuous. Any worthwhile discussion of a manuscript includes the ideas it provokes, and it behooves the writer to sooner or later become aware of what those are.

→ What is the story—or the chapter—about?

→   Does the writer seem to begin with one idea and then veer into something unconnected?

→   Do the elements listed above contribute to your understanding of the theme, or does the writer's choice of details, style, characters, and other elements confuse you?

TITLE:

→   Does the title of the story or novel contribute to your understanding of the pages you've read?

→   Does it offer a "key" as to theme, or how the author might intend you to read the manuscript?

After you've pondered these elements, heft your pencil or pen and get to work. Reread the manuscript, marking places and phrases that worked for you and ones that didn't and—this is a great help to the author—write commentary in the margins as to why. This is an opportunity for you to communicate directly with the author, and a great exercise in figuring out why you like or dislike certain kinds of writing.

Some readers like to create a key: a check mark or some squiggle lines for something that is particularly effective; a question mark beside something that doesn't make sense; parentheses

> The more thoroughly you apply yourself to the task of intelligent criticism, the more your perception of writing will expand.

around a phrase or section that seems redundant and can be deleted. I had a reader who would write, simply, "Fix" in the margin of a bad section, or, cogently but less helpfully, "Snore."

I ask the students in my own workshops to write a paragraph or two giving their overall response, and some participants come to class with a page of typewritten notes—an act very much appreciated by the author under discussion. But however you go about this preparation, at least determine a thesis of sorts: what you did and did not like about the story, and about the writing. This will ensure that you **generate an opinion before you come to workshop**. It will keep you from being swayed by what seems to be the "overall consensus" of the workshop, all too often the view of one or two articulate and opinionated participants.

These prepared critiques will also force you to examine what you think good writing is, as well as why you think so. You will need to substantiate your thinking with specific examples. Specificity and detail are as vital in criticism as they are in writing.

It is helpful to first address what you think the writer is doing <u>well</u>—what it is about the manuscript that you think "works." When it's time to discuss the manuscript's less successful attributes, be respectful. Don't rewrite the story. Your criticism and suggestions should address what already exists, with the goal of making it as good as possible. It helps to keep this idea in mind: what was the writer going for? How well did she accomplish what she set out to do?

Some of the participants in your workshop may be working in a particular genre—historical fiction, "chick-lit," romance, speculative fiction (sci-fi), fantasy. Avoid any tendency to precede your critique with, "I never read this sort of thing," or "This isn't my cup of tea," comments that immediately create defensiveness in the author as well as in those whose cup of tea such fiction happens to be. Our job is to take what's on the page and make it effective—that is what everyone is there to accomplish. Remember, literary fiction is a genre too.

The person whose manuscript is being critiqued is depending on your attention and looks forward to the insights which you, specifically, have to offer. For this reason, flip, sarcastic comments are not welcome, neither in class nor on the page. It is all too easy to be arch and wryly brilliant while demolishing someone else's writing. In writing workshops, as in every other path of life, the Golden Rule applies.

Be sure you sign your name to your critiqued manuscript. At the end of his or her workshop the writer gets these back and it is helpful to relate written criticisms to what got mentioned (or, as often happens, what did not) during class discussion.

If for some reason you are not called upon in a workshop to voice your opinion, it is up to you to raise your hand and do so, especially if the class consensus is moving in a direction that diverges from your own. All too often, the writer being workshopped gets her critiqued manuscripts home and, upon reading through them, discovers that what seemed to be the opinion of many was actually the (loud) determination a few. Speaking up is part of being a "good" (meaning productive and contributing) workshop member. It is a responsibility. If you feel something is being praised too highly or—particularly— criticized too much, dare to say so! Sometimes the discussions that erupt from these disagreements can be explosive, but they are almost always illuminating.

It is also possible that in the course of a good discussion you might have your mind changed.

For the purposes of discussion, it is extremely useful to **talk about the writer and the work being critiqued in the third person**.

This takes a bit of getting used to, but it is a worthy discipline. The author does not have to feel, as author/teacher James Frey puts it, as if he is in the docket answering charges. Rather than worrying if he's acknowledging the person who's speaking, or demonstrating that he's "taking" it well, the author can concentrate on listening to the criticism. This keeps criticism from being given—or taken—personally, and encourages a discussion of literature, rather than a personal "take" on the work under examination.

Never assume that something written in the first person, or even third, is autobiographical. Never address the writer as if he is the narrator (as in, "I was troubled by that section in which you slept with that awful woman").

FOR THE WRITER WHOSE WORK IS BEING DISCUSSED:

Above all: *Listen* to what is being said. **Do not enter into the discussion of your manuscript.** Even nodding or wincing or shaking your head may alter important perspectives which might not, as a result of your reaction, be articulated.

Bring a notebook and jot down the important points that come up during class discussion. This serves several purposes. It will help you remember excellent ideas that might otherwise slip away in the heat of the moment—and it can get hot. It can also help you keep from getting defensive. (You can scribble your snide comments into the notebook.) In addition, when the time comes to rewrite, you can refer to these notes.

> The goal in your workshop is not to explain your story, but to witness what readers are getting out of what you put on the page.

It's very important that you **do not defend your story**, even to yourself, much less out loud. If something isn't clear to your readers then you must rest assured that it is not in your manuscript, no matter how obvious you may think it is.

After a workshop is over, you might want to take a clean or relatively unmarked copy of the manuscript and cull the comments your readers have made onto this one copy. When the time comes to rework the piece you have all the criticism in one place. This also gives you an opportunity to examine all the responses together and see where there is a consensus of opinion. However, sometimes one reader may mark a passage, "YES!!! LOVE THIS!!" and another might draw lines through the same section and write, "DELETE THIS—IT BUMPS ME RIGHT OUT." In this case—and it happens often enough—there is clearly something exciting going on. It is up to you to decide what's caused the variety of reactions. While it may be the result of something confusing, it may also be something from which the story may actually benefit.

If possible, give yourself some time away from a story or chapter section before beginning a rewrite. While this is not always feasible, sometimes the space and time allow the dust to settle. You will find yourself remembering and synthesizing the salient criticisms, often the ones that were the hardest to hear, and forgetting those which are not vital to your rewrite.

And remember, it is your story. You must keep in mind what you are going for and stay true to that endeavor. Sometimes it's a tough balance, but it's worth fighting for: listen well, but keep your own counsel.

REGARDING NOVEL SEGMENTS

WHEN READING A NOVEL SEGMENT:

Unlike a short story, which is a self-contained unit, a novel segment cannot and should not answer all of a reader's questions. In fact, a novel must consistently accomplish the opposite of this: generate enough mystery that the reader continues to turn the pages.

We need to keep this in mind as we critique a section of a novel. The lack of resolution in these pages may very well be part of a longer arc the author is purposefully creating. Often the questions we wonder about—why does Margie get mad at Jim when he mentions babies; why does Phoebe keep thinking about her sister; why does the author include sections about a tortoise making its way across a road—are exactly the ones the author wants us to ask. Creating the desire to know what happens next in the essential task of the novelist.

However, this is not the same as confusing the reader. If you find yourself wondering whether or not the writer has thought of certain issues, mention them! Certain ramifications of plot, character, image, metaphor, and other elements may not be clear to a writer until they have been pointed out. Sometimes these revelations are exciting and feed the direction in which the book is already going. Sometimes they create the need for the author to re-think and re-write whole sections. The author may be appalled at what certain readers think items or activities signify. On the other hand, she may be deeply gratified that her readers are "getting" what she has so carefully layered into her manuscript. Readers' insights of this kind are invaluable.

If a novelist is making you want to know more, acknowledge that he is doing so. Similarly, let him know, respectfully, if he is not succeeding at this essential task.

FOR THE PERSON RECEIVING CRITICISM ON A NOVEL SEGMENT:

Again and again you will be tempted to say, "Oh, that's in the next section," or, "I covered that in the Chapter Three." If the questions brought up in workshop do happen to be answered elsewhere, nod sagely and pat yourself on the back: you've done your work. If the questions raised are ones that startle you, or the ramifications are different than what you intended, try not to get defensive. In either case, **Listen. Take notes.** Ideas will be presented that you haven't considered and that you might be inspired to include.

Sometimes issues are raised: "This moves slowly, there's too much unneeded detail." "The character seems strident." "The writing is choppy." It's probable these criticisms are pertinent to the novel or to your writing as a whole. Try to take the specific criticism and apply it to your work in a general way.

REGARDING WORKSHOP LEADERS, AND THE OCCASIONAL "BAD" WORKSHOP:

Difficult though it may be, particularly if your workshop leader is famous, and/or articulate and/or opinionated, remember that his or her opinion is only one opinion, albeit at times a highly experienced one.

Workshop leaders are expected to have done their own preparation and have usually developed their own style and methods. It is not uncommon to set up the class so that the discussion moves around the room, with each participant in the workshop offering an opinion. This is important, even vital, for the first several manuscripts, but once the members of the workshop have warmed up to each other and to the work at hand, the discussion may take on its own momentum. If some participants stay quiet too long they may be asked a question. It may be easier, if you are shy, to sit back and let the voluble do the talking, but that is not what you are in workshop to do. You are there to probe and discuss and realize your own opinions about what makes a piece of writing work, and this takes active participation.

You may get a workshop leader with whom you have an immediate affinity; you may have one who seems downright mean, and of course, anything in between. Sometimes lessons are hard learned. I think it's possible to get them without being devastated. But if your workshop is "tough"—and sometimes, no matter how good the intentions of all involved, it can be—take heart. There is probably a good lesson in there somewhere.

Every workshop leader has something very particular to say about the process of writing. Something can be gleaned from every workshop and every teacher. Sometimes a workshop that seems harsh at the time will result in a series of valuable improvements in your writing.

Which leads me to say: Sometimes we come to a workshop and offer up our manuscript as if it is our very heart. Sometimes our life seems bound up in the three to five thousand words we present to our peers. But do not expect that everyone, or even anyone, will see in your pages all the care that you have lavished there. We can feel destroyed by the casual— no matter how respectful—attention our pages may receive. Be prepared for this. Your life will probably not change as a direct result of your workshop. But, if you pay attention to the critique of your own manuscript, and are careful and thorough with your critiques on the manuscripts of others, your writing will change, and then, perhaps, your life will too.

Writers' workshops, writers' conferences, can be very intense times. Souls are often exposed—in stories and around those manuscript-littered tables. Sleep well. Eat well. Take care of yourself, and of your peers.

IN CONCLUSION:

Jane Austen did not scribble several copies of *Pride and Prejudice* for her family to mark up and critique. Nevertheless, a distinguished discussion no doubt took place around that Austen tea table. In our efforts to help each other we are continuing an honored tradition. We are in the fortunate position of bringing our respective insights and experience with writing and life to bear on each other's work.

A workshop may be ongoing: a group of writers who live in close proximity and meet every few weeks, a course that extends over days or even a semester. When working with your peers you have the opportunity to come to know one or several whose opinions and insights you particularly respect, and who seem to understand what you are trying to do with your writing. Perhaps this one, or these few, may be willing to continue to work with you. If you don't live in the same area, you can exchange manuscripts by mail, e-mail critical perspectives to each other, make arrangements to read manuscripts and then talk on the phone. Many legendary literary friendships have sprung up out of this mutual regard. If you are lucky enough to find those who will work with you in this way, you join an honorable tradition.

An effective workshop is usually the result of collaborative hard work. It is also tremendously exciting and sometimes even fun. It requires discipline, especially in a week-long conference, when in addition to lectures, readings, ancillary outings, and spontaneous talks with staff and fellow participants, you must critique at least two manuscripts a day. But those who thoroughly apply themselves to the task of intelligent, careful criticism begin to appreciate how writers *work*. They uncover techniques, ideas, connections that invariably illuminate their own writing.

This has been a revelation to any number of workshop participants. They tell me that while it was interesting and helpful to receive responses to their own manuscript, what they actually garnered from the workshop process was **the development of their own critical faculties.** These gleanings of art and of craft, and above all *the ability to criticize a manuscript effectively*, will be applied, in the future, to their own work.

Pay attention. Take care of each other. Use no adjective that does not reveal something. Avoid abstractions. And have a great workshop.

LESSONS FROM A TOUGH WORKSHOP,
OR
THE BACKPACK

During my two years with the Iowa Writers' Workshop I spent a semester with Frank Conroy, at the time the Workshop's director. He quite liked a chapter of my novel, but later in the semester he gave a story of mine some scathing criticism. He read my dialogue aloud, calling attention to its banal nature (it was indeed banal) and pointed out the incessant number of details I used. He called the style in which it was written, "Abject Naturalism."

Now, the word "abject" summons up for me the image of a Victorian woodcut in which a father stands in a doorway, a long, accusatory, and damning finger pointed at his daughter, who is hunched over a pregnant belly, shawl across her weeping face. And it's raining. And as Martha Graham, the pioneer of modern dance, has said, "All art is distortion." Clearly, "naturalism," especially used in this context, was a reprimand regarding my excessive use of (banal) detail.

To give some idea about how right Frank was (and he proceeded at, I guess you could say, abject and detailed length to make his case): The point of view character in the story has just had an abortion, and she's traveled alone to the Southwest to visit some friends. I tried to show rather than tell the reader the complicated background, with (I thought) sly references to the doctor-like fingers of the friend who picks her up at a bus station; drawing attention to the bloodiness of the chicken they prepare to barbecue; the shining implements with which the meat was turned and poked. My understanding was that detail shows, therefore, detail is good, and I used lots of it.

After the workshop—hurt, aching, furious—I went through the pile of manuscripts that had been handed back to me by my fellows. I realized that while not everyone thought the story was as dreadful an effort as Frank had made it out to be, one particular margin note was extremely telling. With no sense of irony a fellow student had written: "It *does* take a long time to cook chicken on a grill, doesn't it?"

This sympathetic comment did a great deal to point out to me the actual nature of my writing problem. I pinned a piece of paper to the wall above my desk, large block letters shouting,

"BEWARE ABJECT NATURALISM!"

I imagined the novels I would publish, and the blurbs that would ride across their shiny hard covers:

Sands Hall, founder of the school of Abject Naturalism, has done it again!

*Here is another of Hall's triumphantly ba-
nal novels, filled with the exquisite minu-
tiae of life's mundanities!*

It took months before anything about that lecture or that devastating workshop began to sink in. But when it did, its infiltration into my writing process was thorough and widespread. In his lecture Frank had said, "As a story begins, the author makes a tacit deal with the reader. You hand them a backpack. You ask them to place certain things in it—to remember, to keep in mind—as they make their way up the hill, that is, through the pages. If you hand them a yellow Volkswagen and they have to haul this to the top of the mountain—to the end of the story—and they find that this Volkswagen has nothing whatsoever to do with your story, you're going to have a very irritated reader on your hands."

The analogy of the backpack and what we ask the reader to put into has become very useful: what do we ask the reader to observe, to remember? These must be se-lected—revealed—with care. I devised for myself a filter through which a detail needs to pass: does it forward some-thing about character? And/or plot? And/or theme? Does the detail manage to contribute something to the development of all three?

This was a great lesson, and (she admits, grumpily) worth the pain it took to learn it.

SOME ESSENTIALS

Here are a few notions that are (according to me) essential to the kit we carry with us as writers.

In the first place: All stories, of whatever length, are made up of scenes. All scenes must take place somewhere, in a setting.

Usually our characters are doing something: an activity.

Activity often involves some objects; if it doesn't, these are still around our characters, ready to be put to use to reveal some aspect of personality or emotion.

Every writer knows all this implicitly. But we don't always take advantage of what we can purposefully do by putting these elements to work.

SETTING, ACTIVITY, OBJECT

Where do we place a scene? What are people doing? What might they be handling? Much can be signaled to a reader through these decisions. Scott expertly negotiating white water in a kayak is very different than Scott revealed at his computer in the stark cubicle that is his office. They may both reveal aspects of the same Scott, but which does the most work for you? Which does the work you want at that particular point in your story?

We are always engaged in activities. If we're not, in our current culture, the *lack* of activity may speak volumes. Wanda watching television while squirting dollops of Cheese Whiz straight into her mouth illustrates one kind of character; Wanda ironing linen napkins may reveal another aspect of her nature—or someone else all together.

Objects, whether or not they are incorporated into the selected activity, can help reveal character—and plot— and theme. As a visitor (along with the reader) is shown into a living room, his attention is caught by a book called *Healing with the Angels.* A flute lies on the table next to some sheet music. A half-empty bottle of Macallan's Scotch stands beside the couch. Do these objects reveal one complicated character? Or a trio of unlikely roommates?

Setting, activity, objects can be used to imply information, rather than explicitly stating, Charlotte's despair at her failed career as a flautist was evident in her desire to believe in angels and her dependence on excellent Scotch to get her through the day.

OBJECTIVE & OBSTACLE

In any given scene, the characters involved must have something they want. There must also be something in the way of getting what they want. This creates tension, conflict, necessary to a good story and to an effective scene.

"Give a character an obsession and turn him loose," Ray Bradbury has said. As we go about creating a story, it is essential to ask, "What does my character want?" It may be money, a child, love, status, revenge, success. As we hone in on what it is, the scenes we need to include will come clear, and the objectives in a particular scene will usually mirror these larger ambitions.

The obstacle, that which is in the way of a character's ambition, her heart's desire, helps create plot. If a character could get what she wanted, there would be no story. Obstacles in the way of achieving money might include a background of dire poverty and no education, or an inability to save. In the way of a child is no man, or infertility. Keeping her from love is something in her own nature. Out of these obstacles we build the plot that will allow her to get what she wants—or, as if often the case, not to get it, or to get it in an unexpected way, or to get something else, unexpected but satisfying.

SELECT & REVEAL

✳ Any detail, to be included, should <u>reveal</u> something.

> **Reveal**:   To make known (something concealed or secret).
>
> To bring to view, show.

This word derives ultimately from words that mean "to pull back the cover," an image that seems a slow rather than a sudden process—after all, reading happens sequentially, one letter, then one word, then sentence, paragraph, page at a time. We have to determine which detail conveys what kind of information, and in what order we reveal that to our readers. This process involves <u>selection</u>.

> **Select**:   To take as a choice amongst several; pick out.
>
> Of special quality or value; one that is chosen in preference to others.

Selection involves having a reason, a purpose. As writers we know intrinsically that putting a character in a Volvo will convey something about their nature, just as finding them in a pick-up, a jeep, or a Porsche will convey something quite different. The more we delve into the craft of writing, the more useful the word <u>purpose</u> becomes. What is our intention? If we keep that in mind—what the story is about, what we want to convey—certain writing problems begin to clarify.

A WRITER IMPLIES; A READER INFERS.

imply: to express or indicate indirectly.

infer: to reason from circumstance, sur-mise.

              to lead to as a consequence or conclusion.

When we say that a speaker or a sentence <u>implies</u> something, we mean that something is conveyed or suggested without being stated outright. <u>Inference</u>, on the other hand, is the activity performed by the reader or interpreter in reaching a conclusion that is not explicit.

A writer implies. A reader infers. Our job as writers is to supply those inferences, as it is our job, as readers, to discover those implications.

Writers can be amused or appalled at what readers infer. Peter writes a scene that takes place in a kitchen: as a couple chats away, the wife merrily chops vegetables and throws them into a wok. "That's their marriage," says one reader, "Hot oil!" and as Peter shakes his baffled head another colleague argues that the wife clearly hates her husband: "Look at the way she's chopping those carrots. Whoa! Bit of a phallic symbol there, wouldn't you say?"

I once put a story up in workshop in which it happened to be raining, and in which two boys happened to be named David and Jonathon. To my astonishment, a workshop peer went on at length about the story's biblical ramifications. I only wish I'd been as brilliant as this reader made me out to be—and have certainly looked closely at the implications attached to the names of characters, as well as to weather, ever since.

Implication requires purposefulness: we need to know what we want our readers to "get." While it may take some preliminary work to uncover this information—and sometimes, in spite of all the "pre-writing" in the world, we uncover it only by putting our characters into action and by having them talk to each other—identifying that purpose makes other choices much easier. And a great deal of fun. If the forty-five-year-old character in a story trades in his Volvo for a red Porsche most readers will immediately know—infer—something about that man.

SARAH AND HER MORNING BEVERAGE

Scenario #1: We find Sarah in her kitchen. The clock on the wall says 5:30; the sky outside the window is the white-gray of dawn. Sarah lifts a bag of French Roast from the cupboard, grinds the beans fine, tamps a loaded spoonful of the stuff into the filter of a complicated espresso machine. She froths her milk in a cup with a matching saucer, adds the espresso, and carrying her beverage, leaves the kitchen.

When I describe this scenario, drawing attention to the fact that it contains setting, activity, and objects, I ask what might be inferred from these details.

Sarah has no children!

is usually one of the first answers. Others include:

Sarah likes good coffee.

She has money! She has time!

She's anal! No, she's just meticulous. No,
she's pampering herself.

She likes nice things. She likes ritual.

Scenario #2: Sarah enters her kitchen and lights a flame under a kettle. Again the clock says 5:30; again our attention is drawn to the early-morning light. While the water comes to a boil, she spoons loose-leaf chamomile tea into a earthenware pot, adds the boiling water, and carrying the pot and a ceramic mug, she leaves the kitchen.

She's a hippie!

is usually one comment.

The idea of enjoying a ritual comes up again. The aspects of Sarah's nature that are <u>inferred</u> from this scenario include a discussion of drinking chamomile tea first thing in the morning:

She's mellow!

She's organic. She's healthy.

She's relaxed. She's calm.

Or trying to get calm.

Scenario #3: Again it's early. Sarah races into the kitchen and turns on the spigot full-blast, shoving the handle all the way to the left, to "hot." From a cupboard she pulls down a jar of Taster's Choice, shovels three tablespoons of the instant coffee crystals into a cup, adds three tablespoons of sugar, tests the water to see if it's hot, shoves the cup under it, stirs the mixture, and flees the kitchen.

Sarah's got children!

She's a student! She over-slept.

She's got a high-pressure job.

*She's in a rush. She needs to get some-
where, but needs caffeine even more.*

These scenarios could be used to reveal three different characters named Sarah. They could also be used to
reveal tension in Sarah's life: She is confronting something
that disturbs the routine that the cappuccino ritual demonstrates. One morning, news comes that her beloved uncle
has had a stroke; the instant coffee shows the urgent need
to get to the hospital. The tea comes after several nights by
his bedside and a need to get some sleep.

By giving our readers an opportunity to delve into
the "clues" we leave for them, we allow them to engage
with our material in meaningful ways. They reach in, they
solve, they figure out; we ask them be smart (which all
readers are capable of being, if we trust them). When we
have a good sense of what we intend the reader to infer, we
start to have fun with the writing. This sense of purpose
helps us eliminate extraneous detail, especially on rewrites,
as elements of our stories become ever more clear. When
we do the necessary work of understanding what we want
to convey to our readers, our writing takes a giant leap
forward.

A FINAL ESSENTIAL: Read. Write as often as you can,
with purpose. Critique the work of others. And read some
more. Keep an eye on what the writers are doing. Take that
to your own writing. Examine the work of friends, or published work. Read.

PUT IT TO WORK
EXERCISES:

1. Lists of Three (page 217)
2. Establishing Character (page 219)
4. Searching for Significance (page 223)

ON THE SUBJECT OF
LETTERS AND LITERARY

It still astonishes me what these simple black marks on a white page can accomplish. Squiggles, really, that we've imbued with significance, which, depending on the language, march up and down or across a page, creating words, which create sentences, which create pages full of paragraphs, which allow us to see a field of daffodils, understand a concept, hear and smell a carnival; they make us laugh aloud or put a book down, drop our head back against a sofa, and sob.

What is that miracle?

Words.

Words that are made up of letters.

The letters of our English alphabet are for the most part abstract, but I like to consider how the curves of our S, and its sound, descend from the shape and sound of <u>snake</u>. I like to imagine that our W, when its curves are rounded and elongated, might have once been a sign for wave, or water, and that even its sound, in some stretch of the imagination, might be one that water makes: wh. And how precisely the mouth sounds and shapes an O. But mostly, letters are signs, signals to our minds to put them together with other letters to make words that contain significance, connected to other words to create further significance….

The root of the word LETTER comes from ANIMAL SKIN, HIDE. I imagine a muscle rippling along a forearm as a hand holding a piece of bone, or a piece of metal, scratches marks onto a piece of tanned bearskin, and hands this to a runner, who sprints across a distance to deliver it to someone able to decipher those marks:

WE ARRIVE IN 3 MOONS.
BRING 7 COWS.
I ∑Δµø∏ YOU.

Letters. A letter.
Letters are the symbols we etch onto hide and parchment and vellum and paper and computer screens. A letter is also a document, written to another, composed of a hundred, a thousand of those smaller letters. A letter gets written to share an experience, an emotion; at its heart lies a desire to communicate something to another; and a story might be seen as a letter, to a reader, telling them something they did not know before. Telling them something they knew but that perhaps they didn't trust someone else did too; that's always a comfort.

As we express ourselves ever more clearly, insightfully, vividly, truly, we get more literary, a word that descends from letter. We explore vocabulary, employ verb tenses, and wield punctuation—a word that shares its root with piquant (a way to spice up our letters). We exercise grammar, a word that descends from glamour. (Imagine syntax being so popular that to employ it well was deemed glamorous.) We use nouns that name. Verbs that move. Adjectives that describe. And we exert other literary devices: Tone and diction. Sound and form. Rhythm and alliteration and allusion and allegory. We invent other voices to write our letters. We get more literary. We get more grammarous. We ply symbol and simile and metaphor, manipulating images that ask our reader to conjoin two unlike things so as to convey deeper and more complex understandings.

And that—conjoining images to convey more complex understandings—is what I want to talk about next.

CAPITAL M METAPHOR

Metaphor and simile reside in that large basket of word choice called "figures of speech."

The phrase, "a large basket," is a figure of speech—an image, a <u>figure</u>—that allows a reader to visualize the idea that, like eggbeaters and spatulas, simile and metaphor are nestled or jumbled in with other image-creating tools, such as symbol, hyperbole, and personification.

The concepts of simile and metaphor are usually introduced together—in grade-school English, in high-school Lit—and while they are not interchangeable, they offer similar pleasures and can be employed in similar ways. Both rely on the same concept: <u>a word or phrase that ordinarily designates one thing is used to designate or conjure another.</u> A comparison is implied or—in the case of simile—stated. These tools make our writing come alive. They create pictures in the reader's mind. They engage the imagination.

✓A simile usually uses "like" or "as" to make a comparison clear for the reader; a well-caught simile is a delight.

The Mississippi Delta was shining like a National guitar.

"Graceland," Paul Simon

The heat of the sun was like a blanket; it had dimension and weight.

Warlock, Oakley Hall

... his handwriting reminded me of untied shoelaces.

Beach Music, Pat Conroy

A ring of trees encircled the field, coastal trees, wind-bent and gnarled yet still symmetrical, like figures straining to balance heavy trays.

The Invisible Circus, Jennifer Egan

✓A metaphor is less specific in its comparison; it asks the reader to do some work, to supply the image.

I could drink a case of you and still be on my feet.

"Case of You," Joni Mitchell

. . . but lately my hopin' machine's been a little on the blink.

"Bound for Glory," Woody Guthrie

Dwell I in the suburbs of your good pleasure?

Julius Caesar, William Shakespeare

The fame of Leadville silver eclipsed Dead-
wood's promises of gold; the new camp was
booming at an altitude of ten thousand feet,
close to the ridgepole of the continent.
                A Victorian Gentlewoman in the Far West
                                    Mary Hallock Foote

As is the case with many derivations, the root of
metaphor is a metaphor. The word ultimately comes from
the Greek. Its prefix, *meta*, means, among other possibilities, change. (We see it used in the word metamorphosis: *meta* /change + *morphe*/form: to change form.) In the case of metaphor, we have *meta*/change + *pherein* /to carry, or to bear: thus TO TRANSFER. Buried within the word is the idea that metaphor carries change with it. It carries its ability for transference.

"Upon disembarking into the bustle of Piraeus," writes my friend Tom Taylor, "we puzzled our way through sights and sounds of a new language and alphabet. Among the first words I sounded out from the Greek alphabet was METAPHOR, painted on various trucks and vans hurtling about the seaport. I chose to believe that these were moving trucks, transforming lives as they transported chattel. Carrying change! Bearing transformation! It was a moment of memorable resonance; I had discovered a literal metaphor."

Metaphors are in use around us all the time, and an enjoyable and useful exercise is to look for and note them down. Driving around, listening to your radio, is a great place to start. Song lyrics use them all the time. A friend who is a songwriter writes about the *roadmap* on her face, and sings that *it's the detours that etched some of these lines.* A sexy ballad from World War II informs us that the singer has *the deepest shelter in town.* A country tune uses puns to make its point: parents are remembered as *so in love*; the mother is depicted while mending clothes—she was *sewin' love*; the father while planting and harvesting—he was *sowin' love*.

Familiar adages supply visual images that may have once made literal sense and still metaphorically do: *A stitch in time saves nine* describes fighting newlyweds who decide to see a marriage counselor. When a new managing director comes on board a struggling arts organization, no doubt the *new broom sweeps clean*. *Pulling out the stops*—what an organ-player does to create a huge sound—might describe the efforts taken to prepare a party for a close friend. Long after adages have lost any relevance to our lives we continue to use them. Examples of such "dead metaphors" include the use of *beat a dead horse* to describe a faltering campaign pouring millions of dollars into advertising. *Rule of thumb* comes from an ominous source: the law that allowed a man to beat his wife, as long as the stick was no larger in circumference than his thumb.

Many advertisements take advantage of the power of a visual "transference" of meaning. Absolut Vodka's ad campaigns are a series of clever visual puns, including one that includes a pile of wrapped gifts at the base of a sparkling Christmas tree beside a bit of baseboard that sports a little mouse hole in the shape of a miniature Absolut bottle; the subscript reads, "Absolut stirring." (As in, "Not a creature was…") Another shows a bottle covered in—it's visual, so the viewer is forced to consider the significance visually—red tape, with the subscript, "Absolut D.C." Marlboro offers luscious photographs of men and sunset and horses in Canyon Country, meant to convey the taste—and by extension the life—available to you if you will just use this product: "Come to where the flavor is."

A newspaper's sports page often offers pun-filled headlines that conjure visuals: BRUINS ROAR TO VICTORY; CANNON SPARKS N.U. LOSS; CUBS MAUL CARDINALS. A friend who has a hard time shifting quickly from one task to another tells me that he doesn't have *a good clutch*. The apt and unusual use of a noun such as this one is captivating, and worth the work it takes to find apt ones. More common—so common that we often don't realize the force they have on our mind's eye—are active verbs, and these are the ones to put to use in our writing. A man can walk into a party, but how much more evocative if he *slithers*. A refrigerator can stand in a corner; it could also *loom*, *squat*, or *hum*, supplying an emotional resonance for the scene.

In the following poem, Margaret Atwood uses a quaint and charming simile to begin a description of a relationship:

> YOU FIT INTO ME
>   by Margaret Atwood
>
> you fit into me
> like a hook into an eye
>
> a fish hook
> an open eye

The second stanza, in addition to turning the loving simile on a very nasty metaphorical ear, implies a great deal of clarity about the situation: the recipient of the hook—whatever the hook represents—has her eyes open; furthermore, it would be hard, with that barbed bit, to jiggle out or pull away or otherwise disengage the hook of this marriage.

"What happens to a dream deferred?" asks Langston Hughes:

HARLEM
by Langston Hughes

What happens to a dream deferred?
Does it dry up
like a raisin in the sun?

Or fester like a sore—
And then run?

Does it stink like rotten meat?
Or crust and sugar over—
like a syrupy sweet?

Maybe it just sags
like a heavy load.
Or does it explode?

To answer his initial question, Hughes strings together a series of similes, But for the final image—and ultimate answer—of the poem, he leaves it to the reader to imagine what a dream deferred might explode "like," and in the process makes the last line stronger than if he'd supplied the image.

Seamus Heaney's lovely poem "Digging" starts with a simile but in the process of the poem—about a writer choosing the life of a writer—the image itself not only changes, but is presented to us at the end as a metaphor:

DIGGING
by Seamus Heaney

Between my finger and my thumb
The squat pen rests, snug as a gun.
Under my window, a clean rasping sound

When the spade sinks into the gravelly ground.
My father, digging. I look down
Till his straining rump among the flowerbeds
Bends low, comes up twenty years away
Stooping in rhythm through potato drills
Where he was digging.
The coarse boot nestled on the lug, the shaft
against the inside knee was levered firmly.
He rooted out tall tops, buried the bright edge deep
To scatter new potatoes that we picked
Loving their cool hardness in our hands.
By God, the old man could handle a spade.
Just like his old man.
My grandfather cut more turf in a day
Than any other man on Toner's bog.
Once I carried him milk in a bottle
Corked sloppily with paper. He straightened up
To drink it, then fell to right away
Nicking and slicing neatly, heaving sods
Over his shoulder, going down and down
For the good turf, digging.
The cold smell of potato mould, the squelch and slap
Of soggy peat, the curt cuts of an edge
Through living roots awaken in my head.
But I've no spade to follow men like them.
Between my finger and my thumb
The squat pen rests.
I'll dig with it.

When I discuss this poem with a class of writers, some find it disturbing that the poem begins by likening a pen to a gun. But perhaps Heaney is asking the reader to ponder one of the things a pen can do, which is to wield words as a form of violence. The poem also begins with almost doggerel-like rhythm and rhyme, which is how jingoistic slogans can be chanted and remembered. "Hell no, we won't go," "Bam bam, bomb Saddam." But "as the spade sinks into the gravelly ground/ my father, digging, I look down," the rhythm slows, "to where his straining rump among the flowerbeds..." and rhyme is abandoned; the poet/ persona appears to turn to more interesting matters as the father: "bends low, comes up, twenty years away..." and Heaney has delivered us neatly to the subject of his poem.

And now he puts more subtle writer's tools to work. He employs most of the senses: the sight of his father's "straining rump"; the sound of "the squelch and slap of soggy peat" (alliteration, too, to make us hear it); "the cold smell of potato mould" (and, in using one sensory perception to describe another, he employs synesthesia); the feel of those potatoes, "their cool hardness in our hands." He also puts active verbs to work, many of which have to do with the subject and overarching metaphor of the poem: dig, root, scatter, nick, slice, heave. He also uses a flashback—or a loop, as I like to call such shifts in time and place—taking us, via that "straining rump," back to the father, who digs for what his family will eat, then back further to the grandfather, who, digging turf, supplies a material that can both house and warm. Then the narrator returns us, as a good loop does, to the present tense of the piece—"through living roots awakens in my head..."

At this point, in a phrase that indicates the respect he has for his forebears, the narrator tells us that he has "no spade to follow men like them." Yet through the work of examining their digging, and through writing the poem, he has decided the best use to which he can put his pen is not as a gun, but to pursue, in a metaphorical way, the occupation of his ancestors: to use his pen to delve into his history, his culture, his life: "I'll dig with it."

"Digging" exemplifies what I call a capital, or Big, M Metaphor. Small m metaphor is a figure of speech—those that allow a reader to see a figure, a form, an image. Capital M Metaphor is the overall meaning that we are incorporating into a piece of writing, often usually reflected by, or attached to a small m metaphor.

Big M Metaphors move beyond and encompass more than the place given to the figure of speech described in style books. A Metaphor can be the skeleton upon which an entire poem, essay, story, or novel rests. It can be argued that the word "symbol" is adequate to describe these larger ramifications, but a symbol by definition is static— "usually a material object representing something invisible" —and symbols are usually given to a reader in

> For in truth, story writing has much in common with bullfighting. One may twist one's self like a corkscrew and go through every sort of contortion so that the public thinks one is really running every risk and developing superb gallantry. But the true writer stands close to the bull and lets the horns—call them life, truth, reality, whatever you like—pass him close each time.
> Virginia Woolf

the form of nouns: the whale in Melville's *Moby Dick*, the cathedral that the narrator and the blind man draw in Carver's "Cathedral," Frost's diverging roads.

Metaphor, however, implies an ongoing transformation. It is dynamic. It is interactive—something that unfolds between artist and audience, writer and reader. A successful Metaphor is a process of discovery and cognition. This process often takes place over the course of an entire piece of writing; its resonance is affected by further elements of the metaphor falling into place.

Thus Metaphor can "carry change" in another way. In the course of Ibsen's play, *Peer Gynt*, onions are planted, harvested, peeled, sliced, chopped, added to stews and sandwiches; the audience understands that onions are not only useful and tasty, but that Gynt seeks them out to add spice to his sometimes-banal life's soup. As the play unfolds, the onion takes on a different significance: the onion—an object that has no center—comes to represent the meaningless life and empty heart of the protagonist. Effective writers intend objects, activities, settings, characters, and almost always their titles, to resonate on at least two levels. (Shakespeare's *Hamlet?* No; Faulkner's *Hamlet?* Yes. Austen's *Emma?* Maybe not; Connell's *Mrs. Bridge?* Absolutely.) If a reader mentally tugs at the object, reflects on the activity and setting, ponders a character's name or the title of a piece, he will as often as not find connections among these and the ideas the piece is presenting. When we write, we reverse this: We layer in— overtly, subtly—elements that will allow our insightful readers to receive the several interpretations we are providing.

A whale, a cathedral, two roads are transformed when something about them, or around them, becomes active. If symbols are nouns, perhaps metaphors are verbs. They (or we) "transfer" these meanings; they carry, or bear, change:

It is the *chasing* of Moby Dick—not just the whale itself—that is the driving force of Melville's novel. The pursuit allows us to fill in what the whale may represent. The setting of Ahab's ship and the ocean on which he travels are part of this extended metaphor of the frustrated longing that can give life meaning.

In Carver's "Cathedral," the narrator *draws* a cathedral for a blind man whose fingers "ride along," and in the process the narrator comes to understand something about being inside something built—however it is built—to house grace. That they are sitting on the floor, while a TV drones static into the tacky living room of the narrator's house, offers ironic resonance (depth): grace can be found anywhere.

One of Frost's roads is not *taken*. The acts of *diverging*, of *choosing*, of *traveling* (and of not traveling), activate this poem. When the poem's message begins to take form within us, the setting—the yellow woods, the path whose leaves "no step has trodden black"—adds to our comprehension.

What one reader chooses to think the whale, the cathedral, or the roads represent may well differ from the ideas of another reader. This is part of metaphor's charm—and occasionally frustration. But the writer should have a good idea of what he intends. Robert may not know why, in his story about an elderly and childless woman, he has named her Martha, or why, when a sister visits and chatters on too long about her grandchildren, he has Martha boil their morning eggs until their yolks are rock hard and almost inedible; but Robert should figure out the significance of these things—and put them to work—by the time he's ready to send the story out for publication.

In her essay "Living Like Weasels," Annie Dillard writes that weasels get hold of what they want and don't let go. "One naturalist refused to kill a weasel who was socketed into his hand deeply as a rattlesnake," she writes. "The man could in no way pry the tiny weasel off, and he had to walk half a mile to water, the weasel dangling from his palm, and soak him off like a stubborn label..."

"...like a stubborn label" is a powerful use of simile, and with "socketed" and "pry" Dillard puts verbs to work as metaphors.

In the essay, Dillard describes a walk she takes; she sits on a tree trunk, "ensconced in the lap of lichen, watching the lily pads at my feet tremble and part dreamily over the thrusting path of a carp..." Then, behind her, a weasel emerges from a wild rose bush. Observe the intense figurative language she puts to work as she describes this encounter.

> Weasel! I'd never seen one wild before. He was ten inches long, thin as a curve, a muscled ribbon, brown as fruitwood, soft-furred, alert. His face was fierce, small and pointed as a lizard's; he would have made a good arrowhead. There was just a dot of chin, maybe two brown hairs' worth, and then the pure white fur began that spread down his underside. He had two black eyes I didn't see, any more than you see a window... Our eyes locked, and someone threw away the key.
>
> Our look was as if two lovers, or deadly enemies, met unexpectedly on an overgrown path when each had been thinking of something else: a clearing blow to the gut. It was a also a bright blow to the brain, or a sudden beating of brains, with all the charge and intimate grate of rubbed balloons. It emptied our lungs. It felled the forest, moved the fields, and drained the pond; the world dismantled and tumbled into that black hole of eyes. If you and I looked at each other that way, our skulls would split and drop to our shoulders. But we don't. We keep our skulls. So.

What Dillard seems ultimately to be writing about, using tools she manipulates exquisitely and precisely, is the act of being a writer. Her *need* to be a writer. She imagines what it would be like to become a weasel, sinking into a place where she would live underground, in a nest, not having to emerge except for food. As the weasel chooses

what it wants and "does not let go," so she does: she writes.
And in this essay, as if to prove this point, she pulls out the
stops: simile, metaphor, hyperbole; a precise description of
the place she is sitting, and the mood she is in. The writing
might not be everybody's cup of tea—I have students who
strenuously object to the idea of teeth being "socketed"
into skin, for instance, and who find preposterous the idea
that an exchanged glance with a weasel might fell a forest
and drain a pond—but Dillard wants to communicate what
that moment was for her, and what it represents to her, as a
writer. She uses language to force a reader (whether they
want to or not) to be there too, to have the experience she
had. Capital M metaphor.

THE OBJECTIVE CORRELATIVE

No discussion of
Metaphor would be com-
plete without mentioning a
term coined by T.S. Eliot,
the *objective correlative*.

Eliot applied this
term to the technique in art
of representing and ul-
timately evoking a particular emotion by including
physical symbols of it—
environment, activity, action or gesture, sets of objects—that become indica-

> "The only way of expressing
> emotion in the form of art is by
> finding the objective correlative;
> in other words, a set of objects, a
> situation, a chain of events shall
> be the formula of that particular
> emotion; such that when the
> external facts, which must
> terminate in sensory experience,
> are given, the sensation is
> immediately evoked."
>
> Athenaeum
> T.S. Eliot

tive of the emotion and are associated with it.

An author selects and inserts something physical—
something *objective*, tangible in some way—that *relates* to
an issue (theme) addressed in his work. It's not simply a
symbol, though, the meaning of which remains somewhat
static throughout a piece of writing. The significance of an

objective correlative changes as the narrator's view of it does, and it reflects that change—often packing an emotional wallop as a result. In the beginning of Faulks's *Birdsong*, the narrator's sensory perceptions are powerful, and vividly rendered. Eventually, as a soldier in World War I, Stephen spends a great deal of time underground, setting land mines and the like (that subterranean world, void of all sensory perceptions, even light, and certainly no singing birds, signifies the deadening of senses that happens as a result of war). The ending of the book contains a moment when he hears birds again —a tree full of them. It's an uplifting moment for the reader as well as the narrator, as we have been with him through these shifts in perception—including the reawakening of them—and the title suddenly takes on a new resonance as well.

When I teach a class on metaphor I have students look up numerous related words, including:

→ Symbol & Analogy

→ Literal & Figurative

→ Imply, Implicit & Implication (and Infer & Inference)

→ Object & Objective & Relate & Correlation

→ Connect & Connection

→ Sign, Signal

→ Significance.

As readers we are looking for signs; we want them. We like to feel smart, and if an author gives us signs— significance—pointing the way, we are allowed to exercise our faculties to determine where we are headed—it's an enjoyable and mutual process. As writers we want to provide this for the reader.

If Robert finds the eggs in his story significant, he writes the story so that they are to the reader as well. A hook and eye. Roads. Digging. Onions. A hamlet. A National guitar. Drinking a case of you.

When a writer has purpose and intention—and often this clarity does not emerge until our second, seventh, eleventh draft—anything can be selected and utilized as a signal to the reader: where to look for meaning. Writers have to understand significance. We must obsess about significance. And then we put it to use in our writing.

PUT IT TO WORK

EXERCISES:

4. Searching for Significance (page 223)
1. Lists of Three (page 217)
5. Combining Elements (page 225)
6. Checklist for a Scene (page 227)
7. Metaphor *en Scene* (page 229)

SEARCHING FOR SIGNIFICANCE

When I was fourteen, a high-school English class included a two-week tutorial on the poems of Robert Frost. Mr. Holden, who had known Frost personally, waxed eloquent on the poetic devices at work in "The Road Not Taken," "Two Look at Two," "Out, Out—" and many others. Questions on the final exam asked us to examine and discuss a poem we had not covered in class: "Mending Wall."

"Something there is that doesn't love a wall..." the poem begins, and describes two neighbors who meet each spring to rebuild the wall between their adjoining properties. The poem ends:

... I see him there
Bringing a stone grasped firmly by the top
In each hand, like an old-stone savage armed.
He moves in darkness as it seems to me,
Not of woods only and the shade of trees.
He will not go behind his father's saying,
And he likes having thought of it so well.

He says again, "Good fences make good neighbors."

I scratched and erased and huffed my way through the exam's various questions, and then came upon the ultimate poser: "The poet implies the fence is designed to keep something out," it read. "What do you think that is?" Pleased with the speed with which I could answer this one, a little puzzled by how easy it was, and very proud of my vocabulary, I wrote: "Rodents, and other small animals."

A friend and I walked away from class, and paused on a bridge that spanned a small spring-running creek. I was troubled. "That last question was so simple," I said.

My friend gave me a slow look. And something about that studied gaze worked on me. In a blinding flash—and it was like a conversion, a discovery of faith—I received the mantle of metaphor. Nevermore would something be only what it literally was. This search for significance has served me well as writer, director, actor. It can also lead to complicated mental processes: when not being able to find a parking spot represents the futility of all endeavor. Or when the gift of a lovely redbud tree to my mother with the green thumb not only does not flourish but drops all its leaves.

Knowing me, my mother showed me the sad little desiccated shrub and said, "Sands! It is not a metaphor!"

Further thoughts on this: I took that little shrub home, covered with a black trash bag, thinking that perhaps it was high altitude that had done it in. I left it on the deck and, weeks later, went to put it in the trash and found that, rather miraculously, beneath its plastic shroud it had happily come back to life.

Then I forgot to water it.
And it died again.
All the way, this time.
See what you are doing? You are searching for significance.
Believe me, I've exhausted the options. When Mr. Holden returned our exams, I leafed reluctantly to the last page, dreading what he would have written there. But he was kind: "Perhaps you need to look a little deeper, Sands."
And so I have. Searching for significance is now like breathing. And it's also sometimes very irritating. As a Zen master has said: "Sometimes a mountain is simply a mountain." But not when that mountain and that redbud tree are in our novel.

RENDERING LIFE INTO ART

fiction: an imaginative creation or pre-
tense

a literary work whose content is
produced by the imagination, not
necessarily based on fact

a lie

Like other artistic disciplines, writing can be a process through which an artist comes to understand and sometimes resolve issues in her life. If the work is effective, it
may also illuminate these issues for the reader.

In the process of sorting out a personal experience,
a writer is sometimes compelled to tell a story "as it really
happened." But is such a piece of writing fiction? Perhaps
the piece is instead a personal narrative or part of a memoir. Perhaps it might be more aptly shaped as "creative non-
fiction," a form that allows the personal nature of a memoir
to be conveniently mixed with the techniques of fiction. In

fact, the techniques involved in writing creative non-fiction are precisely those used in writing fiction, with this vital exception: The reader is allowed to assume, correctly, that the author is the narrator. In a work of fiction, however, the reader is asked to suspend that assumption. In fiction, it is understood that the author <u>creates</u> the narrator—the person telling the story—and that the narrator/character is <u>not</u> the author. This distinction is useful. The memoirist writes to tell what happened, sharing the realization or lesson that accompanied the experience. While authors of fiction may have a similar intention—to share an insight or perception—they write stories that are by and large products of their imagination.

This does not mean that writers of fiction don't select autobiographical elements and put them to use in their work. They do. Sometimes they borrow bits and pieces of their lives—the memory of a living room, a friend's eyes, dialogue from a phone call—as a way to make a fictional world more vivid. And sometimes they use much more, perhaps in an effort to come to terms with an experience they've had. They delve deeply into the experience not to tell "what really happened," but what they learned as a result.

But it is still fiction the writer is creating. The root of the word, "fiction," comes from the Latin "to form," and that is the fiction writer's task. Forming. Shaping. Selecting. Rendering.

IN PURSUIT OF TRUTH, NOT FACTS

"Early" writers—writers beginning to develop an interest in craft—who struggle to turn autobiographical incidents into fiction often have a hard time hearing that something isn't ringing true, or isn't working. "But that's the way it was," they tell their workshop, or their friends. "That's what really happened!"

Similarly, early writers can lose track of the fact that it is fiction they are reading. You may find a workshop peer aghast that you actually slept with that peculiar man, the very first night you met him!, or walked away from that poor dying cat! or murdered that old lady—with an ax!

The Library of Congress page of most novels contains a phrase that reads something like this:

> This is a work of fiction. Names, characters, places and incidents are the product of the author's imagination. Any resemblance or relationship to characters or events, living or dead, is purely coincidental.

This is meant, of course, to keep those who would read their lives into our stories—and total strangers will—from accusing us of "stealing" their experiences, their histories, their children. The author is saying, "I made it all up; this is not based on anything in the world." Sometimes it's a ridiculous caveat; readers know the story and the characters, they know the author has borrowed lock, stock, and barrel from his own life, or someone else's, or from some source. But the phrase is traditionally placed at the beginning of a work of fiction.

In a prefatory note to his novel *Warlock*, a book that takes place in the Old West, author Oakley Hall purposefully alters the phrase:

> This book is a novel. The town of Warlock and the territory in which it is located are fabrications. But any relation of the characters to real persons, living or dead, is not always coincidental, for many are com-

posites of figures who live still on a frontier between history and legend.

And he goes on:

> The fabric of the story, too, is made up of actual events interwoven with invented ones; by combining what did happen with what might have happened, I have tried to show what should have happened. Devotees of Western Legend may consequently complain that I have used familiar elements to construct a fanciful design, and that I have rearranged or ignored the accepted facts. So I will reiterate that this work is a novel. The pursuit of truth, not of facts, is the business of fiction.

While Hall is talking about the issues that attend the writing of an historical novel, where authors often mix history and fiction, the quote is applicable to a work of fiction in which autobiographical territory is explored — when we write from our own experience we could be said to be writing a form of "historical fiction."

One of the synonyms for the word *fiction* is "a lie." Yet when we set out to write what really happened, we intend to tell the truth. If we replace Hall's phrase "Devotees of Western legend" with, "People who know me," we get a sentence that reads:

> People who know me may... complain that I have used familiar elements to construct a fanciful design, and that I have rearranged or ignored the accepted facts....

This might well describe our fears when we use incidents or characters in our lives as a basis for our fiction. Yet, is our intention to present facts when we write fiction or, as Hall suggests, are we attempting to discover or reveal truth? The story "Rashomon" is one incident told from several perspectives. It poses the questions: *Who is "right?" Which perspective is "correct?"* as well as some answers: *No one is. They all are.* Truth is a slippery thing, and our belief in a particular truth often has to do with our trust in who is telling the story. Early in our study of craft it is hard to predict how a point of view may be interpreted by others. What a writer, particularly one incorporating autobiographical material, considers to be "truth" may not necessarily read that way. Your effort may be to show that the man building sandcastles with a group of children is struggling to regain his youth; and be horrified to discover—especially if your own delightful experience with children on a beach is what inspired the story—that because of details you've included, half your workshop assumes he's a pedophile. And if they're not wise to the idea of fiction, they may consequently assume that you are.

A more common problem is this: When a writer knows a story intimately, he often leaves out information that must be present if the story is to make sense to a reader. These details may include background material, relationships among characters, the history of an entire family or even of a community. The writer may see his characters clearly but—because they already exist—he does not paint them for the reader. Similarly, the reader is given no sensory impressions regarding the rooms and landscape in which the story takes place. Although these may be vivid in the writer's mind, he has not created them on the page. The reader does not get to see what the author's narrator sees.

Whereas, when a writer is creating a character, a world, out of whole cloth or even out of scraps, she is far more likely to make sure she can see that world clearly, which of course means that the reader does too.

INCIDENT & STORY

Another problem that accompanies a desire to render life into art lies in the difference between an incident and a story.

> After everything that happened, (main character) was never the same again.

An incident, often related as if it were enough to make a story, is an interesting anecdote in which nobody changes. A story is more likely to be that in which the protagonist glimpses something about life, or her own nature, which changes her forever.

Whether an author has too much material to work with, or too little, "telling what really happened" is seldom effective. The author must distill—"extract the essence of"—what the experience represents to him, and render his fiction out of that.

Render has many definitions, but let's look at just two:

> to represent in visual or artistic form; depict

> to reduce, convert, or melt down (fat) by heating.

Render is a useful verb to keep in mind when we are trying to wrest or create fiction from an autobiographical incident or even, simply, from an emotion: heating it with intention and skill and craft, to get the fat off, then shaping it into a work of art.

Once we have made the decision to use a detail or an entire episode from our own lives, we must feel free, as the derivation of "fiction" communicates, to *form* it: to change, reduce, convert the material to our purposes. This idea can also be put to work in the writing of non-fiction. But instead of rendering or inventing, the process becomes one of selecting.

"WRITE AS IF EVERYONE YOU KNOW IS DEAD"

When an author uses a real experience or a family story in her fiction, she can feel hobbled by the tether of what "really happened." It can be difficult to change even the smallest detail if she feels bound to it by courtesy or family ties. Anne Lamott's advice—"You must write as if everyone you know is dead"—while excellent, is sometimes difficult to put into practice.

A solution is to ascertain what you want to accomplish with a particular story—the "truth" you want to tell. You will be much more clear about why certain elements need to stay "as is," and what you will need to alter—not to protect a relative or friend, but in order to best serve your story. Then you can begin to use the material effectively.

Perhaps the facts are that Maria's grandfather married her grandmother at the top of the Grand Canyon at noon, and Maria wants to use that scene in her novel. She likes those details—married at high noon on the rim of the Grand Canyon—because both clarity and risk are so neatly implied: Her grandparents knew what they were getting into. But Maria's grandfather was also a controlling cuss and Maria wants to put that to work in her novel, which deals with issues of patriarchy—she may be inspired by or is working through her own marriage, her upbringing, or simply the culture in which she lives—or she simply thinks she can characterize the fictional grandfather more effectively if she changes a few details. So perhaps she has Grandpa force his fiancée awake to get her to the Rim just as the sun is coming up. This shift of detail allows Maria to not only communicate Grandpa's controlling nature, but allows her to imply the "dawn," for better or worse, of this marriage. Or, perhaps, to imply the darkness that may attend the marriage in her novel (which may or may not reflect the marriage of her actual grandparents) she has them wed at dusk. Whatever Maria ultimately chooses, she chooses with purpose. She knows what she wants to communicate to her reader, and what she forwards—about plot and character and even theme—by dramatizing that scene and utilizing those details in her novel.

Yet too much detail can be a problem. Most writers understand the injunction, "Show, don't tell"; they understand that detail adds color and interest. But sometimes the writer using autobiographical material errs on the side of adding too much. She paints a charmingly clear picture of Roxanne's table, the surface of which is covered with adorable containers of sugar, honey and Sweet 'n Low; an antique pitcher holds cream, another skim milk. A sterling basket, given to Roxanne by her mother-in-law, is filled with individual bags of every kind of tea. Perhaps the author makes it clear that the teapot also belonged to Roxanne's mother-in-law.

The word *significant*, (as well as the word *signal*) descends from *sign*: something is being pointed to, something is being indicated.

With so much space given to these details, the reader assumes they are significant. He may suspect that the story is about Roxanne's inability to make choices, or perhaps about the strained relationship between Roxanne and her mother-in-law. But if the mother-in-law is never mentioned again, if the metaphor of all-the-things-one-can-put-into-tea is not further explored, the reader is left with a lot of detail, charmingly rendered, but with no value to the story. Nothing has been forwarded, and the scene is "wasted." The author is not clear about why she's including these details.

Now, it may be that in that author's real life, her teapot is indeed a gift from her mother-in-law, with whom she is, in fact, quite friendly. And perhaps she does provide all those options for guests when they drop by for tea. Because that is what the author does, she loans those details to Roxanne, without having a purpose for doing so. Why does she select that detail? What does that detail reveal to the reader?

To be effective, the author needs to examine what's she's selecting to show the reader, especially if her own character is similar to the character she is creating. She may decide, "Indecisiveness is at the base of my story." Or, "It's the mother-in-law issue I'm writing about." In the process of examining the possibilities, the author may discover she likes what she can imply with Roxanne's dizzying choices. Perhaps she changes the basket of teabags to boxes and boxes of Celestial Seasonings' teas—Sleepytime, Country Peach Passion, Red Zinger. She appreciates the characterization she can swiftly accomplish as Roxanne selects Tension Tamer and the mother-in-law a bag of Morning Thunder. In the end, however, if the tea and cream don't reflect or underscore what the scene is "really about," our author may simply write, "Roxanne waited until the whistle began to scream, poured the boiling water into the teapot, and with a sigh, set it on the table between them."

AUTHORIZING EVERYTHING ON THE PAGE

Richard Ford was once asked how he knew when he was finished with a piece of writing. His answer: "When I have authorized everything on the page."

That word "authorized" is powerful. Before Mr. Ford puts his work out for others to read he knows the purpose of every single thing he has included. He has selected what's on each page, he knows what every detail implies, the work that s being done by every scene, what the work as a whole accomplishes. He has authorized it.

The word *authorizing* leads us to the concept of authority: Someone who has power, who commands, who adjudicates, who has the final say. When a fiction writer includes autobiographical material, she is still adjudicating. She exerts her authority over what she chooses to include (as well as omit) on each page—and part of that authority is purpose—she knows why she has done so.

Both authorizing and authority descend from author, of course. Someone who originates. Someone who creates. Someone who has formed a piece of fiction whose business is, as Oakley Hall so wisely states, not facts but truth.

PUT IT TO WORK

EXERCISES:

8. My Two Grandmothers (page 230)
9. I Still Believe in Unicorns (page 233)
10. Through Other Eyes (Getting Some Perspective) (page 235)
1. Lists of Three (page 217)
2. Establishing Character (page 219)
4. Searching for Significance (page 223)

Note: A few ways to introduce yourself to and/or create a new character:

→ You might use the exercises to take a look at yourself through other eyes (how you imagine others see you), or at someone in your family, or

→ You could write about what you imagine are the perspectives of people you know about people you know, or

→   Take on the perspective of someone you in-
    vent to look at yourself and others you know.
    (See the discussion of *persona* in "When the
    Narrator is Close.")

IN THINGS

THE EFFECTIVE USE OF DETAIL
IN SHOWING AND TELLING

No ideas but in things.
William Carlos Williams

As writers, we have all heard the injunction "Show, don't tell." The phrase sounds good, but what exactly does it mean? And how does one go about accomplishing it?

Most stories use a combination of showing and telling, or—other words for similar concepts—summary and scene, narrative and dramatization. It's perhaps not so much a matter of "don't tell," but rather, "if you tell, tell effectively": there can be boring showing, as there can be very vivid telling. Previous essays in this volume discuss strong verbs and figures of speech and other techniques to make language vivid, and subsequent essays talk about how these essentials are used to establish and maintain point of view. These tools are used to move purposefully between summary and scene, from narrative to dramatization: from tell to show.

In my mind's eye I see a large gauge, with SHOW on one side, TELL on the other; a needle swings between them. When writing is effective—and this is often a matter of style—the needle is not necessarily stuck to one side or the other, but moves easily across the gauge. Usually we employ "narration," or telling, or summary, when we are effecting a transition between scenes, or in setting up a scene. But such a summary can still be concrete and vivid:

> Joe hadn't seen Mercedes in the ten years since their divorce, years in which he'd flitted from woman to woman seeking a redress for wrongs he could never articulate but which thrummed in the shimmer of candlelight, between 400-count bedsheets, in the smell of an armpit, for Christ's sake, and made each of these lusts close in clouds of flailed resentments. So when he saw Mercedes, looking younger than her now fifty-seven years, a new hair cut making the most of that intelligent chin and forehead, smiling up at the smirking silver-haired fox that was her date, if not, for all he knew, her new husband, he wished he were a cat and could put his belly to the ground and slink out of the restaurant, unseen, growling deep in his throat. Instead, he had to fling a smile onto his face and...

and we move into the scene.

In this case the writer doesn't need or want to "show" those ten years. They are not important to her story; what is important is the scene she is about to dramatize. We will see the restaurant and Mercedes and Joe's respective dining partners as well as what they order to eat and to drink, which will reveal aspects of their characters; some salient details about the missing ten years may be unfolded in dialogue, but the purpose of the scene is not to recap the past but to forward the story.

Similarly, we could take a page to describe the way a character puts his hand on a door knob, turns it, opens the door and watches the crack of light fall across the floor; we could describe how he steps carefully through the opening afforded him and using ample detail, could show him carefully closing the door behind him... But unless this is a Raymond Chandler mystery, in which a lot depends on just how this door is opened and closed, it might be easier (for the author and the reader) if this was stated: "He stole into the room."

So. Narrative, or summary, is an essential and important part of craft. When we move into a scene, when we dramatize, we can establish, vividly, a great deal more: We can find out not only *where* the characters are and *who* they are, but also aspects of relationship and history. And perhaps the most important thing: We don't tell readers this information; we engage them in discovering it.

Readers enjoy the process of picking up the clues a writer has purposefully placed for them to find, and putting them together for themselves. As authors, we create opportunities for that to happen when we put characters in a place, in action, engaging in activities and in dialogue: when we dramatize a scene.

Dramatization allows a reader to see and hear and feel and smell, to be there in the environment with the characters. Much of this is accomplished through the artful selection of detail. Detail moves a scene from the general to the specific. We might write:

> As Jim and Margie sat in Fred's Diner finishing breakfast the tension between them was palpable.

We have just told the reader, using narrative, where the scene takes place and what's basically going on—which is fine as far as it goes and may be all that's needed to launch the scene. Choosing to dramatize the scene not only reveals character and environment more vividly, it allows the reader to infer aspects of personality and relationship:

> "And how are you folks?" The waitress paused beside their table and smiled at Margie. "How's that oatmeal, hon? You need some more coffee?"
>
> "You bet," Jim said, and swabbed up a smear of egg yolk with a last triangle of toast, added a knife-tip of berry jelly, and pushed the wad into his mouth. As he shoved his plate at the waitress he spoke through the mess of toast and yolk and jam. "You can take it."
>
> Margie looked away, out the window, where semis muttered in the parking lot and a woman in red shorts dragged a squalling girl by the arm.
>
> "I said, I'm done." With a clatter Jim added his fork to the plate. Go ahead, *take* it. And bring coffee."
>
> Margie put fingers to her forehead. "Jesus, Jim, you don't have to—"
>
> "Don't start." He yanked a napkin from the dispenser on the table. "I don't need another lecture on how I talk with my mouth full or my table mannerisms that you find so incredibly offensive." He lifted the creamer,

tilted the lid open with a thumb, and sniffed.
"This shit better not be sour."
    The waitress winked, and lifted
Margie's bowl. "Hey, sweetie, did you eat any
of this? You sure you're finished?"
    "That's the way she eats," Jim said,
and pushed his voice into falsetto. "Birdy,
birdy." He wiped his mouth, tossed the nap-
kin onto his plate. "She's done. Believe me.
She's done."

While the effort to dramatize a scene usually takes
up more room on a page, much can begin to be established: the characters and the nature of tension between
them, as well as a sense of place. Because we're in Margie's
point of view, we get a sense of Jim and the diner and, at
the same time, we begin to see who she is through how she
reveals what she sees. This aspect of sense of place is a
useful tool in the building of character and/or a point of
view.

SENSE OF PLACE

    The term *sense of place* has developed a number of
meanings, and at its most basic it is the environment in
which a scene takes place: a room in a dingy tenement, a
beach in California, a spaceship, Vermont woods in fall. It is
the setting, the backdrop, what a reader might see as the
curtain of the unfolding scene begins to rise.
    We can accomplish this by simply telling the reader
these things, even vividly telling them:

    Margie left Jim peering at the head-
lines in the newspaper dispensers and
pushed out of the heat into the diner, where
overhead fans cooled the air. The customer-
noise was almost unbearable, and signs

tacked to the walls urged various specials, including "Try Our Pie!" The thought made Margie feel sick. She headed for a booth with a view of the Interstate, and stared out at the busy on-ramps and off-ramps, which served to remind her, as everything seemed to do these days, of the purposeless knotted mess of life with Jim.

It may suit the author to narrate the set-up of a scene in this way. This is largely a matter of style. But we can reveal character—and develop a specific point of view—by selecting *what* our point of view character notices, and *how* he or she describes what is noticed.

As she pushed through the glass doors into the diner, Margie lifted her hair from her forehead and raised her face to the cool air wafted about by several overhead fans. A waitress waved, "Sit anywhere, hon!"

A trucker at the counter, a wedge of pancake speared on his fork, looked around and wiggled his eyebrows. Margie jerked and peered out the window at Jim's silhouette. He was bent over, reading the newspaper headlines in the dispensers outside. The waitress finished mopping a table near the window and flapped the towel in her direction. "It's all yours, hon."

But a gauntlet of tables, filled with customers, all of whom seemed to be shouting, loomed between her the window, beyond which the gray tracks of freeway sped towards a low-lying smudge of smog. The trucker winked. Margie tugged at her cut-offs. She pretended to be vitally interested in the assorted signs tacked around the walls that urged her to *Try Our Pie!* The cash register rang and clanged.

"TRY OUR PIE!" Jim squeezed her waist with sudden pinching fingers. Margie twisted away from what she knew was an act of ownership performed for the benefit of the leering trucker. She held fingers to her lips to keep down a sudden swell of revulsion and almost staggered towards the booth where the waitress had left two laminated menus the size of small doors. She stared out, through finger-print-smeared glass, at the cars hurtling past on I-70. Coming and going, down the off ramp, up the on ramp, circling, gassing, eating, driving; where were they all going and what was the point.

We get an idea of the "setting" of this scene: the fans, the heat, the noise level, the signs on the walls, the booth near a window that looks out on the freeway. Because we're seeing it through Margie's perspective, we also begin to get some clues about her and her attitude towards her life and towards Jim. Selection of detail helps to do that, as will, now that they are seated, a choice of what they will order (Margie, oatmeal with skim milk please; Jim, eggs, toast, bacon, hash browns, side order of pancakes); how they eat; how they treat the waitress who serves them—in other words, selection of activity and objects.

ACTIVITY & OBJECTS

Much can be shown about characters not only by where you choose to place them, but also by what they are doing and handling. Again, the analogy of a curtain rising to reveal an environment and characters in action is useful:

Where can this scene be set to most effectively reveal your characters—their personalities and their dilemmas? What are your characters engaged in accomplishing (or prevented from accomplishing) as the scene unfolds? These selections can reveal essential information.

Once you have placed your characters in a setting, and given them something to do, a number of objects are available to put to use as well. These "props" (a word from the actor's lexicon) may be utilized to further reveal plot, character, a character's emotions (a good action is worth a hundred words), and even theme.

My work in the theatre, particularly as director and playwright, has allowed me to see how much can be done the moment the curtain goes up, as the lights brighten, or—in fiction—as our reader bends her eye to the page. Where we find people and what they are doing can reveal a great deal to the reader, even before we launch those characters into a scene.

Let's put these ideas—setting, activity, props— together. Let's look at Millie and Bud.

MILLIE AND BUD

We find Millie in her living room. She rocks in her rocking chair, which sits on a rag rug next to a window. Outside the window is a tree…

But what kind of tree? An evergreen might communicate permanence to a reader. A cherry tree in blossom, its white and pink vivid against an aching blue sky, might

"No one can achieve profound characterization of a person… without appealing to semi-unconscious associations… To sharpen or intensify a characterization, a writer makes use of metaphor and reinforcing background—weather, physical objects, animals—details which either mirror the character or give the character something to react to…"
On Moral Fiction
John Gardner

communicate a sense of ambivalent hope. The author may choose to have the window be open, and add in the chirps of a bird and maybe the buzz of a neighbor's lawnmower. But perhaps the author decides, for metaphorical reasons, to plant a deciduous tree: outside the window is an oak whose leaves blaze out against a gray sky; or—Millie is, after all, getting on in years—perhaps its naked branches scrape against, maybe even implore, the winter sky.

The author gives Millie a cup, or maybe a pot, of tea. Earl Grey, laced with milk and honey. Chamomile. Or Darjeeling, or Prince of Wales, which may hint at a faintly British spunkiness. She is knitting. This is a good, if rather clichéd activity for the ninety-one year-old Millie; it's an activity that has to do with Spider Woman, with crones, with those who make stories, forming a substantial something out of not much (in this case, strands of yarn). Her big-knuckled fingers are shown purling and knitting the mufflers—no—the socks she is making for... another choice that will reveal character... AIDS patients in a local hospital. To keep their cold limbs warm.

Then there is Bud. We find him in his garage. Do the walls of his garage sport silhouettes of hammer and screwdriver, and are the tools hung in their allotted places? Is Bud someone who has the detritus of years stuffed in the shelves of his garage? If we decide the latter, we might even describe some of it in order to further reveal who he is: a jumble of broken computers, an engine with parts scattered all over the floor, a 50-lb bag of organic potting soil...

Bud is working on a vehicle. A cherry-red '69 Mustang implies one sort of character. A Plymouth Duster quite another. Ditto a BMW. Let us say that Bud is working on a Ford pick-up and that he drinking a beer (although not a Bud). Maybe a Rolling Rock or Mickey's Big Mouth. A Guinness would reveal something rather different; O'Doul's, a non-alcoholic beer, might hint at something in his past to be taken up later. Will we have him changing the oil (a girlfriend he's getting out of his system?). Or maybe—with the same inner motivation in mind—we have him changing spark plugs. Perhaps, as we put Bud into action we notice he is kind with the plugs, and we are startled to discover that his fingers, though oil-stained, are gentle.

There: Millie and Bud. Rather clichéd looks at two characters who may or may not turn out to be more interesting.

How do we make them more interesting? How might we immediately reveal to the reader some vital element of their natures?

Let's bring that spunky quality of Millie's to the forefront. *She's* in a garage, working on a Ford pick-up. She's suddenly wearing overalls, a few gray hairs escape the red bandanna she's got pulled low on her forehead, glasses slip down her nose as she gets in under the hood and worries a spark-plug out of its nest to test its viability. Millie has a few sparks in her, the reader gathers. And is she drinking a Guinness. Or does she carry that pot of Darjeeling out to the garage with her?

And Bud? Perhaps we decide to emphasize those gentle fingers we spied working on the Ford. Let's place him that rocking chair, drinking Earl Gray, the tree outside the window an orange and red blaze of glory in the fall sunshine. He's knitting socks for AIDS patients; the hope is that the reader will begin to wonder why he's engaged in that activity, and will turn the page to find out.

And back to our poor, squabbling Margie and Jim. Does Jim squash eggs and hash browns onto the back of the fork with his knife? Does he plant his elbows on the table, holding a utensil in each fist, and gesticulate with his fork as he makes a point to our somewhat fastidious Margie? And we can also do better than to tell the reader, "Margie was fastidious." Perhaps we describe how she cuts her toast into small squares, or chews with her lips held tightly together. We give the reader a picture of what kind of people they are and of what their conflicts might be, without having to write: "Jim and Margie were having trouble in their relationship." In addition, our choice to set this scene in a diner off a freeway can be inferred by the reader as a metaphor for, "Jim and Margie had come to a crossroads."

In addition to its many other uses, action helps us to get rid of adverbs, those pesky and ubiquitous "ly" words.

> "So, have you seen Ted recently?" asked Jim, suspiciously.

is perhaps not as effective as:

> "So." Jim chewed for a long moment, squinting at Margie. He'd poured too much cream into his coffee and the liquid had spilled over the rim and onto the table. He lowered his lips to the cup's edge and slurped, then grinned. "How long's it been since you've seen Ted?"

A reader's response to a character is shaped by how and what one character notices about another, which is, essentially, point of view. What does it reveal to a reader that Margie looks away from the flecks of yellow egg she sees in Jim's mouth as he chews? Or that Jim wishes he could wrap his finger in the tendril of hair that curls into the nape of Margie's neck?

We also imply a lot about people by what we have them wear. A silk shirt unbuttoned far enough to reveal a filigree of lace bra shows one thing about a character—as well as something about the character who notices. A character wearing a flowered polyester pant-suit and a pink plastic visor is different from one dressed in a pair of jean cutoffs over fishnet tights and an immense black beret. We can learn things about a character if she wears dark glasses; if she smokes, *how* she smokes; if her clothes are made of natural fibers or man-made ones; even the colors of her trousers. We can also put unexpected clothes on a character—defying whatever cliché might be looming.

What might be revealed through the type and the condition of our characters' belongings? Or the way a character executes a simple action: Does she pick up a delicate teacup by its handle, keeping her little finger extended? Or does she wrap firm fingers around a ceramic mug? These details all reveal, or *show*.

TURNING DOWN THE SOUND

As long as I've incorporated the stage term "props" and the theatrical idea of a curtain rising, here are other similarities regarding the artist who acts and the artist who writes. Both are often confronted by similar problems. Both need to be specific in making choices that reveal character and relationship. Both art forms ask that we not allow ourselves to fall into the trap of what actors call *indicating*, and writers call *telling*, the emotion or attitude called for in a scene. Instead we must find ways to *manifest*, or *show* these things.

A beloved acting teacher of mine, Ed Hastings, once critiqued a scene presented in acting class by asking: "If you turned the sound down on this scene—that is, if you couldn't hear the dialogue—would we still know what this scene is about?"

This question is essential as I work on scenes as an actor and director, and it's become even more important as one of my writer's tools. Taking the time to imagine—and discard, and imagine again, and then create—where a particular scene is set and what a character is doing can accomplish an enormous amount of exposition. Finding a

couple screaming on a roller coaster shows a reader something rather different than finding them walking hand in
hand beside the Thames. Here are the circumstances of a scene I performed in
Hastings's class: A sister and her brother have grown up
under extremely close circumstances. The sister has been
both mother and lover to the boy, and out of financial and
emotional exigencies they have slept together for years. The
sister, older, knows that this incestuous relationship must
stop; the brother does not want it to. Although much of the
scene's dialogue never deals directly with this tension, this
clash of objectives seemed to be what the scene was
"about."

What my acting partner and I had done, in our first
rendition of the scene, was to sit on two chairs and talk—
urgently—to each other. Intellectually we understood the
scene, and we took it for granted that our flashing, averted,
widened eyes and our sometimes subdued, sometimes
histrionic, voices would do what was necessary to make the
scene convincing.

But Hastings informed us that we were "talking
heads" (a phrase reserved for soap operas, and therefore,
considering our lofty dramatic sensibilities and aspirations,
a pejorative). "You're acting up quite a storm," he said,
kindly enough. "Indicating all kinds of terrific emotions.
But you're not manifesting any of them. Turn down the
sound. Let me see what the scene is really about."

Chagrined, my acting partner and I took another
look the scene, this time turning down the sound. What,
we asked ourselves, might these two characters be doing
that would make sense in the context of where the scene
was set (an apartment), and would still communicate to an
audience, if they couldn't hear the words, the nature of the
tension between the siblings?

We finally hit upon the idea (and this brainstorming takes place in a writer's mind as she faces her computer screen, or soaks in a bathtub, takes a walk, wherever and however we do this necessary work) of having the brother and sister return to their apartment with a load of clean laundry. We set the scene in the bedroom and our activity while we spoke the lines of the scene was to make the bed with the clean sheets.

This enabled us to physicalize (show, don't tell!) the characters' objectives as well as their emotions: the brother wants to get his sister to play with him, he wants to get her into bed; the sister needs to let her brother know that their sexual relationship cannot continue. The actor playing the brother could refuse to tuck in his side of the sheets, could pull me onto the bed, wrap me in the blanket (showing not only amorous intentions but his "youth" and "playfulness"). As the sister, I could actively refuse these advances, push him off the mattress, be resolute about tucking in the sheets, folding the extra blanket... No reference was made to sheets or beds in the dialogue, yet as actors we could reveal emotion in the way we handled the props (sheets, pillows, pieces of laundry): The brother shoves his socks in the drawer with his jeans and slams the drawer shut; the sister primly relocates the socks to their correct location.

Dialogue does not and should not always directly address the conflict in a given scene. But turning down the sound can help a writer communicate what a scene is "really about."

Mending a broken plate in a messy garage. Planting a flowerbox on a balcony in the Projects. Sitting in a rocking chair letting out the seams of an antique wedding dress. The careful selection of place and activity helps the writer reveal character and character needs. Even a character's history can in this way be effectively communicated to the reader, while the writer avoids the pitfalls attached to "exposition." In addition, objects and activities allow us to access metaphors and objective correlatives that underscore our themes while simultaneously forwarding character and plot.

SAM AND SUE

Imagine you're developing two characters, and showing rather than telling the reader what you want revealed about them. Sue may interrupt Sam as he is repairing a broken chair. Does she start handing him tools, without being asked? Or does she sit by and watch as he performs his task all by himself—even if he clearly could use some help? If he asks for her help, the way in which he asks has the potential to reveal something about them. Is this an old, comfortable friendship? A budding romance? A marriage on the skids? A peace-making attempt after an argument the night before? Each of these could be illustrated in the way Sam asks for the glue and the way in which Sue does or does not give it to him. Much can be revealed through activity and dialogue, without the author-as-narrator actually telling us the characters' history.

These activities, the ways in which the characters go about accomplishing them, and the objects themselves, can be utilized as metaphors for larger issues and themes in your work. For instance, perhaps the chair Sam is fixing is one of a set he and Sue bought the first year of their marriage, and mending it is an act of re-connection in a marriage that has splintered. Or perhaps the seat and the rungs of the chair can't be fixed, and the two characters, without ever talking about it, come to acknowledge—in a scene that seems to be about handing tools and talking of mundane affairs—that whatever the chair represents can't be fixed either. Or the chair is the first effort of collaboration in a new love affair. (Building and fixing are the rather obvious metaphors here.) This is an excellent layer to keep in mind as you explore possibilities for setting and activity; it can actually assist you in your choices.

For an example of a writer putting these ideas to work, let's take a look at the beginning of Anne Tyler's *Ladder of Years*:

> This all started on a Saturday morning in May, one of those warm spring days that smell like clean linen.

That Delia, Tyler's point of view character, knows what clean linen smells like, and that she makes this simile, immediately tells us a great deal about her. Tyler has selected this detail, along with others in the opening of this book, to allow—even force—the reader to infer various things.

The verb select means "to take as a choice among several; pick out." As soon as we decide to put our character in a setting, engage her in an activity, give her objects to deal with, we must pick out, or choose, these things. We base these selections on our effort to communicate something about our character.

We find Delia, for instance, in the supermarket, where she has gone "to shop for the week's meals..."

> She was standing in the produce section, languidly choosing a bunch of celery. Grocery stores always made her reflective. Why was it, she was wondering, that celery was not called "corduroy plant"? That would be much more colorful. And garlic bulbs should be "moneybags," because their shape reminded her of the sacks of gold coins in folktales.

With the help of that simile, a day that "smells like clean linen," and the knowledge that Delia is "standing in the produce section," the reader gathers that Delia is a housewife, and an organized one (doing a week's shopping). She is also fanciful; she wants things to be a little more "colorful"; and she has old but not-forgotten roots of romance—the reference to folktales. All of these first impressions will turn out to be true as the novel unfolds.

Tyler has placed Delia in the produce section of the supermarket (significantly different information would be communicated if we found her in *canned goods*, or next to the *meat* counter). She is choosing vegetables that might help make a meal flavorful, even spicy: celery is mentioned, as well as garlic, scallions, shallots. When a man presses in a bit close, asking her advice about vegetables, Delia finds this man's hands are not only "agile" but "spidery," a revealing comment, considering the relationship that follows this first encounter. Tyler keeps Delia's activity (shopping) and a sense of place (the produce section) alive as the scene unfolds.

> He said, "Would you know if these are called scallions?"
>
> "Well, sometimes," Delia said. She seized the nearest bunch of celery and stepped toward the plastic bags.
>
> "Or would they be shallots?"
>
> "No, they're scallions," she told him.
>
> Needlessly, he steadied the roll of bags overhead while she peeled one off. (He towered a good foot above her.) She dropped the celery into the bag and reached toward the cup of twist ties, but he had already plucked one out for her. "What are shallots, anyway?" he asked.

> She would have feared that he was try-
> ing to pick her up, except that when she
> turned she saw that he was surely ten years
> her junior, and very good-looking besides.

Since the man is indeed picking her up ("just pre-
tend we're together," he asks her, in order to fool his estranged wife), this is Tyler's sly way of revealing to us that
not only is Delia attractive, but also that she doesn't think
she is. As Delia walks beside him, pondering this odd request, she hears "King of the Road" over the supermarket's
sound system. Here, too, Tyler has made a specific and
purposeful selection; as the plot unfolds we discover that
this organized housewife unexpectedly "hits the road"
herself, abandoning her settled, unflavorful, life. In less
than two pages the reader receives a great deal of tacit
information about why this character will walk away from
her seemingly happy marriage. "Well of course," Delia says
to the man's request.

> And without even taking a deep breath
> first, she plunged happily back into the old
> high-school atmosphere of romantic intrigue
> and deception. She narrowed her eyes and
> lifted her chin and said, "We'll show *her*!"
> and sailed past the fruits and made a U-turn
> into root vegetables.

We spend the rest of the book discovering that Tyler
fully intended that double underscore: the "U"-turn Delia
makes, and the "root" vegetables into which she sails (passing the "fruits" of her life in the process). Even her character's name—short for Cordelia, the daughter that King Lear
most dotes on and by whom he is most infuriated—has
been picked out with care: in the course of the novel Delia
deals with the recent death of her father, and choices made

because of or in spite of him. Tyler's details are folded effortlessly into the narrative, supporting and revealing aspects of her characters, plot, and thematic concerns. They have such specificity and purpose that they seem inevitable.

ATTRIBUTING DIALOGUE

All this talk of setting and activity and objects is of course en route to putting our characters into a scene in which they will usually, sooner or later, talk to one another, and here are a few thoughts about how to attribute that dialogue:

Often the reader understands who is speaking by reading:

> "There you go again," Jim said.
> "There I go again what?" Margie asked.

This is a simple and workable and almost invisible way to keep tabs on who's talking. Unless used judiciously, however, it can get a little repetitious. To solve this, some writers reverse the order:

> "There you go again," said Jim.
> "There I go again what?" asked Margie.

or even,

> Said Jim, "There you go again.

These often only serve only to call attention to themselves. Another "solution" is to use a "talking verb" and/or to add an adverb:

> "There you go again," said Jim, dryly.
> "There I go again what?" asked Margie, defensively.

While occasionally useful in helping the reader imagine the tone in which dialogue is spoken, adverbs can be simply a lazy way of telling rather than showing the character's attitude or tone of voice. Writers also use verbs to describe the way dialogue is being uttered. Using an occasional "Margie grumbled" or "Jim insisted" can give the reader a fair sense of tone. But the good effect wears off fast; these should not be used too much, or too often. Overuse can unintentionally amuse the reader.

The most effective way of showing how dialogue is to sound to the reader's ear is to present character IN ACTION—which is where this all this discussion of setting and activity comes into play. We might write:

> "Oh go to hell," Margie said, setting her cup down, hard.

OR:

> "Tell me what it is, then," Jim said as he leaned back, crooking an arm over the back of the booth.

Better yet, we can delete these "saids" and go straight to the action:

> "Oh go to hell." Margie set her cup down hard, splashing coffee onto her t-shirt. Her fingers trembled as she stuck a corner of a napkin into her water glass and daubed at the stain. "It isn't what you think."
>
> "Tell me what it is, then." Jim leaned back, crooking one arm over the back of the booth. Smoke from his cigarette curled lazily into the air above his head. "I'm interested to see how you plan to talk your way out of this one, Marge."

Jim leaned back gives the reader the implied "he said," which is deleted. *Margie set her cup down hard* lets us sense the tone in which this piece of dialogue is uttered. But this technique, too, can be overused. Attaching some activity to every line of dialogue can be, again, unintentionally, humorous.

And sometimes, there is a rhythm to the use of "he said"—a sense of a space or a pause in the midst of an ongoing dialogue, which is exactly what we want the reader to "hear" as well, and in that case we put it to work.

Further discussion of the pitfalls surrounding dialogue, as well as some helpful hints to avoid them, can be found later in this volume.

EXPANDED NARRATIVE, OR LOOPING

It is a well-known notion that incorporating sensory perceptions into a piece of writing adds depth and vividness to the sense of place. It also helps create and sustain point of view: utilizing the senses in a given setting, or attached to activity or objects, provides an opportunity to delve into and reveal a character's thoughts, emotions, and memories.

This can be thought of as "expanded narrative": combining the kind of information a writer can communicate quickly with narrative with the dramatic potential available from dramatization. The writer "anchors" the reader to the setting—to a sensory perception about the place, an activity, or an object—and then takes his character on a mental discourse in which information about a character's past, philosophy, emotions can be communicated. (This is sometimes called a "flashback," sometimes "inner thought"; I prefer the descriptive term "loop.")

Such movements in time can sometimes confuse a reader. But when we establish an activity for our character in present time, out of which she floats into thought or memory, the reader moves easily with her. When the time comes to return to the present, we effect this smoothly by bringing focus back to the activity in which the character was engaged as the memory or thought process began. Sensory perceptions can be used in this same way. Senses influence our thinking and our memories and can be used both as impetus and anchor.

SIGHT:

To spite her, she was sure, Jim exhaled a plume of smoke across the table. He tapped the cigarette against the ashtray, then rotated it, pressing the glowing nib into a point. The insignia stamped on the bottom of the ashtray, obscured by ashes, looked a little like a dragon, and Margie thought of a book she'd read as a child, in which a dragon with a long green tail and red eyes had wrapped itself around a hapless maiden. But that dragon had charmed the maiden. The maiden had come to love its embraces. The cigarette rotated and Jim tapped it with his index finger. An ash flaked off. He took a deep drag. "Penny for your thoughts," he said, and the smoke poured out of his mouth, dragon-like.

SOUND:

Jim stirred his coffee, racketing the spoon against the cup. Her lips twisting into a moue of irritation, Margie folded her arms and looked away. He'd succeeded in irritating her, a thought that caused him to stir more vigorously. Willy Nelson's moony voice whined above his head and he suddenly longed for his drums, where he could be the one making all the noise, sitting right inside cacophony, surrounded by Morgan's raucous rhythm guitar, the screeching leads of Zeb, and the underlying pulse of Beatty on bass. He set his cup down on the saucer with extra zeal, watching with satisfaction the lines that twitched across Margie's forehead as she tried to ignore it.

SMELL:

Margie breathed in the aroma of toast, buttered toast, overwhelmed with a sudden need to go home. But not to the apartment in Los Angeles—she wanted her father behind his newspaper and her mother in her down-at-the heel slippers and the yellow curtains above the sink and the pop-up toaster. Never mind that her father now had a different wife and that her mother lived in a condo in Florida. Margie wanted to sit at the wooden table waiting for the bread to jump, wanted to breathe in the smell of her mother's cigarette and pungent perfume, wanted to eat over-toasted, over-buttered white bread and then lie on the couch while the TV crooned.

TASTE:

Jim swallowed more tepid coffee, hoping to erase the residue of runny eggs and slimy conversation. Margie hadn't drunk much of hers. She hadn't touched much of anything, this whole stupid trip. She also, as promised, hadn't said a word about the "kid thing," but that didn't mean it wasn't on her mind. As if that was the answer to their

many problems. Ha! He stared at her, at the
high cheekbones, more pronounced than
usual with the weight it suddenly occurred to
him she seemed to have lost, at the blonde
hair in need of a wash pulled back too-tightly
from her forehead. Maybe she was pregnant.
Maybe that was the cause of all the emotional
baggage they'd been hefting in and out of the
car the last few days. The thought made him
choke. A small spray of milky coffee made it
about halfway across the table. Margie looked
at him, startled. In spite of himself he mut-
tered, "Sorry."

Touch:

The Formica table, sticky under
Margie's elbows and forearms, made her
think of the child who might have sat there
that morning. A little girl, perhaps, in a
booster seat, who'd used the syrup dispenser
too liberally, or whose pancakes slid on to
the table en route to her mouth. She looked
away from Jim's moist too-large lips sliding
over a bite of eggs. How had she ever
thought, ever desired, that they would make
a child together?

"Leave it out," he'd said that night, as
she was heading to the bathroom to deal with
diaphragm and spermicide.

She'd paused, sitting on the edge of the
mattress, the floor cold against her bare feet.
He took her hand and pressed it against his
chest. His heart knocked against her palm.
She shook her head. "It's probably not a good
idea," she whispered.

"Sure it is. Now get back in here."
And she'd slid beneath the blankets he
held aloft, slid her body alongside his, her leg
along the lean length of his, his hipbone
against her own. His heart had seemed to
want to escape his ribcage; it fluttered and
banged before he moved her face into a position so he could kiss her.

Her forearms made a faint sucking
sound as she lifted them off the table.
"Sticky," she said, although Jim wasn't listening. He was staring out the window, en-
tranced no doubt by the glittering parade of
cars reconnecting to the freeway.

ENDOWED OBJECTS:

A technique borrowed from the theatre that a writer
can put to work is to endow objects with some history or
special significance. This serves as a way to build the biography of our characters, and allows the writer, like the
actor, to create a rich inner life for them.

An actor may do this with objects on stage, whether
or not the props are mentioned by the playwright as a part
of the set or as part of a character's history. For example,
the script may call for a samovar; it may be an essential part
of the action of the scene; the playwright may have a character refer to it as a birthday gift from a cherished uncle.
This actor might endow the samovar with the memory of
that birthday party, inventing the circumstances and details
of the day, as well as imagining a few of the thousands of
times the samovar has been used. The actor playing this
role might develop other memories: She might invent circumstances in which her dress (which in fact has been
designed and created for this production in the theater's
costume shop) is a hand-me-down from her sister, a fact

she resents. The tea cup from which she's drinking is chipped from an evening a few years ago when, moved to tears by the passionate recitations of a visiting poet, she dropped it; the pillow on a sofa is one she embroidered herself and, proud of it, she constantly turns it so people might notice her handiwork.

This means that everything on stage with the actor has significance; everywhere she looks she is reminded, even jarred, by associations that remind her of and reinforce her character. This actor "homework" means that the things that surround them onstage, whether built in a prop shop, bought at the Salvation Army, or donated by an antique store, are ENDOWED with a history, or significance.

As writers, we can put this idea to use: If you look around your environment, you will see that many of the objects in your room have some history or significance attached to them: The Book of Tao, inscribed by an ex-lover, in a nearby oak bookcase that was purchased with money earned from a magazine article; beside it sits the tiny pewter cat given by a fellow feline-o-phile, and across the room, tacked to the wall, is a postcard bearing beloved writing advice... It's only a small step, as we create our characters, to begin to fictionalize histories for real objects, or real histories with fictionalized objects, and eventually ("no ideas but in things"), fictional histories for fictional objects: We invent needed significance to forward character, plot, and thematic concerns.

Kate is about to hand a glass of Jim Beam; no, Bushmills; no, Glenlivet to an interesting new gentleman in her life, Sam; no, Malacai; no, Alistair (you can no doubt infer the associations I might be making with each of these choices). Kate knows little about Alistair, but likes what she sees so far: tall, intelligent, British, stylishly dressed. We might take time to think about the possible significance of this glass, and how can we endow it so that we develop

Kate, (and Alistair), the plot we're forming, perhaps even thematic concerns?

We might "discover" that the glass is the last of a set that was a wedding gift (the object in Kate's hand suddenly changes from the weight of mere glass to the heft of crystal). Her ex-husband, Dirk, broke all the rest in drunken tirades. The glass has a chip out of its rim which she hopes Alistair will not notice. The author as narrator, or Kate as point-of-view character, might briefly reflect on this as she hands the glass to Alistair. Alistair may ask (or, if we're in his point of view, may wonder) about the sudden dip in her ebullient mood. Perhaps the other glass available, or the one Kate chooses to use, is her son's green plastic dinosaur mug. We might use this to establish (showing not telling) that Kate has a son, as well as Alistair's reaction to that information. Without pointing it out directly, we can let the reader know that perhaps Kate and Alistair are, like the glasses, mismatched; by showing that Kate does not point out the chip in the glass to Alistair, we might imply that she keeps dangerous secrets; from Alastair's insistence that he drink from plastic, the reader may infer that he is perhaps the gentleman Kate's been hoping for…

We might be able to establish a great deal without writing, "Kate had suffered through an appalling number of fights with her ex-husband, a man overly fond of Wild Turkey."

Although, in the end, we may realize the scene is not necessary, and that a narrative sentence is all we need.

While detail is almost always interesting, it's easy to include too much. The reader can be weighted down with pieces of information that are simply not intrinsic to the story you are telling, forcing the reader to haul, as Frank Conroy has said, an unneeded yellow Volkswagen through the story. Still, it is easier to delete then to add, and I'm a great believer in the magic that can emerge in a "shitty first draft," as Anne Lamott calls them. We never know what we might inhibit, or even kill, if we don't allow our imaginations to run rampant. Upon rewriting these pages we might discover that although we don't wind up including this scene between Kate and Alistair, writing it has attuned us to explore history and motivations that serve the story.

To be effective we must select the details we eventually use with care. We need to keep in mind what we may be signaling to the reader with our choices. But as you write, let your mind pursue all possibilities; don't edit them out before you try them. Especially if you are new to the joys of detail, indulge yourself for awhile and see what opens up for you. If you are adept with and understand the power of detail, hone the skill to include only what's necessary. Know why you have included it, what purpose it is serving. Concentrate on choosing details that will be significant to the attentive reader.

Narrative, dramatization (and their cousins, summary and scene), and expanded narrative are tools with which to tell a story. The careful selection of detail is basic to all three, allowing the reader to be in the scene with your characters. Telling keeps a reader at a distance—and, by the way, can be purposefully used to do exactly that. When we show, we bring the reader close, anchoring him firmly in our characters' lives.

PUT IT TO WORK

EXERCISES:

THE LOOP

Flashback: An earlier event inserted into the normal chronological order of a narrative.

Webster's

At a certain point in a manuscript it may seem necessary to let the reader know some of the reasons a character—let us call her Jane—is driven to behave the way she does.

Sometimes this is simply a mental discourse of some kind. Often, however, for the sake of keeping dramatic action flowing—continuing to show rather than tell the reader what is motivating Jane's actions—the author will drop her back in time, taking the reader along. In order to depict an earlier, formative experience that shaped her present behavior, the reader is presented with a flashback.

Some writers leave flashbacks out of their work entirely, preferring to communicate needed information through implication. And it must be pointed out that often flashbacks are a method for the author to discover information about her characters that may not ultimately be needed in the published manuscript. Flashbacks should be used with purpose and discrimination; like everything else in a manuscript, they are included because they are necessary: something essential is pushed forward in this way. Bear in mind too, that sometimes the information contained in a flashback can be more effectively presented to the reader through bits and pieces of dialogue, fragments of memory, allusions to the experience by other characters—techniques that allow the reader to put this past information together for themselves. Also be careful that your "backstory" is not so loaded and so vital that in fact you should be starting your story before, or as these events take place. (As a fellow teacher and writer, Sandra Scofield, wisely says, "Chronology is your friend.")

However, once those drawbacks and cautions have been taken into consideration, the flashback can be useful literary tool.

A memory rarely manifests as a sudden image "flashed" upon the reader's consciousness. To "flash back" may describe how it feels, but is only occasionally how shows up on the printed page. These journeys into time are often extended for at least a paragraph; sometimes it takes pages of dramatization to illustrate an incident and its effect upon the character's psyche.

Such movements in time can be confusing to a reader. "Where am I?" they may ask, meaning not only **Where** am I?, but **When** am I?

Some writers solve this by using a space break (sometimes even a chapter break) to separate the past tense of Jane's flashback from the present tense of her story. Jane might also recall a past incident because it is thrust into her consciousness by something she is presently doing. The source of her recollection might be an object. Or a smell or a sound; senses often stir our memories. Whatever we select to spur the memory, it is useful to ground the reader in the present before beginning the journey into the past or into thought—whatever it is that will take her from the present tense of the scene. One way to accomplish this is to have Jane involved in an activity, dealing with an object, aware of a particular sensory perception, before she is stimulated to recall this earlier time or to reflect on something germane to the story or her character. When she "returns" from recalling (re-living) this episode in her life, the reader finds her still engaged with the present-tense activity, and is immediately able to pick up the threads of the ongoing story.

Grounding the reader in something physical in the present moment can serve another purpose: An opportunity to reveal something significant about Jane to the reader. She's climbing a tree behind the home of her childhood, a house she hasn't visited in decades. She's sprinkling pinches of saffron over a dish of paella, sipping wine and talking merrily to friends in her kitchen. She's filling a dozen hand-made fabric frogs with rice for a local arts-organization fund-raiser. What she is doing, and how she is doing it, give the author opportunities to develop character, plot, as well as thematic concerns.

Clearly the senses are bound up in this. The author gives the reader the feel of the rough bark against Jane's hands as she climbs; the smell and the color of the saffron and seafood, the taste of the wine, the heat of the kitchen; the weight and heft of those stuffed frogs. The reader is anchored with these details in the present tense of the story.

Having anchored the reader in these ways, the writer takes the reader on a "loop." Short or long, a loop of memory can narrate or dramatize a scene that reveals information about Jane's past. As she climbs the tree she remembers running away into its branches when she was five—as she wishes she could run away from her marriage, now. The use of saffron is connected to the lessons learned while cooking with a beloved and deceased grandmother; the laughter a rare moment in a life that's been recently troubled. The slide of rice through her fingers leads her to think of it being tossed at her wedding, which leads to memories of her husband and the mysterious life he led while they were married, which only became clear when he was diagnosed and then died of AIDS.

These thoughts are not limited to memories; they can be musings about life, opinions about another character, a character's epiphany.

Memory or musing, the loop is closed when Jane is pulled back to the present: her husband calls from the back door of the childhood home, wondering where in hell she's got to. The friends in the kitchen want to know if they can open another bottle of wine. Rice spills from the unclosed leg of one of the frogs, and Jane finds her needle and thread and wearily begins to sew it up.

Much fiction is written in the past tense. A tacit understanding exists between reader and writer that events related using the past tense are actually unfolding as if they were happening in the present. When we use simple past tense in the present-day narrative, and continue to use simple past tense as we drop back in time, the flashback may be awkward:

> After dinner, Michael headed into the study to work on his brief and Jane started in on the dishes. She was surprised to come upon the steak knife amidst the clutter of flatware in the sink. It was one of a set of six—she remembered that they came in a

wooden box—that Jorge gave to her for her
birthday, only weeks before they broke up,
and then claimed they were his and insisted
on taking with him when he left. She smiled
with a certain grim satisfaction, recalling
how she managed to slip one out of the box
while he was outside packing his car. Now,
as she washed it, she wondered how Michael—who set the table—found it. She used
a fresh towel to polish it dry, and then replaced it at the very back of the second
drawer, where she hid it, and where it
stayed, ever since Jorge's departure.

Perhaps you were tempted, as you read this, to in-
sert a "had" here and there before a verb to make the transitions into the past more clear. This is something we do
quite naturally, even when we don't necessarily know the
name of the tense we are using. When we use only past
tense, as in the example above, it is easy to get confused
about where—when— we are supposed to be. We are
tempted to rely on words like, "remembered" and "recalled" to make it clear that we are in the past, and phrases
like, "Now, as she…" to make it clear to the reader we are
moving forward in time again.

With judicious use of the past perfect tense, we
lower the reader effortlessly into and back out of the character's memory or mental processes:

She still felt a grim satisfaction that
she'd managed to slip one out of the box
while he was outside packing his car. As she
washed it, she wondered how Michael—
who'd set the table—had come to find it. She
used a fresh towel to polish it dry, and then

replaced it at the very back of the second
drawer, where she'd hidden it, and where it
had stayed, ever since Jorge's departure.

I asked a friend why this tense might be called the
past *perfect*. He said that perhaps it had to do with the
French word *parfait*, which, in addition to meaning perfect, also means complete. So this is a tense that implies
that an event is "perfectly"—as in completely—over and
done.

Some writers, in order to show the power that a past
event may wield over a character, put the remembered
incident in present tense. (For an example, see Amy Tan's
"Half & Half.") Writing in present tense, it is easy to indicate a move back in time by dropping into, then coming
back out of, simple past tense.

The next time you become aware as a reader that
you have just traveled through a flashback, look back and
notice how "had" accompanies the verbs in the first few
sentences. Usually—if the flashback is of any length at all—
this drops out for the middle section of the loop, and then,
as we are coming back to the "surface" of the memory or
the thought process, the writer usually gives us a few more
"hads." This alerts us—this is all quite subconscious—that
we are returning to the present. In addition, be aware of
what it is the author has managed to show you in the
course of the scene or memory—what do you know that
you didn't before?

Here's an example from Anne Tyler's *Ladder of
Years* (ellipses indicate where for brevity's sake a few sentences have been omitted). What's been established is that
Delia has purchased a romance novel, *Moon Above Wynd-
ham Moor*: Watch where Tyler uses the past perfect and
where—even though we are still back in time—she lets

simple past tense do the work, then gives us "had" to return us to the present:

> ... she continued toward Belle's, taking quick, firm steps so that anybody watching would think, *That woman looks completely self reliant.* But there was no one watching. She remembered how, as a child, she used to arrange herself in the front yard whenever visitors were due. She remembered one time when her great-uncle Roscoe was expected, and she had placed her doll cradle on the grass and assumed a pretty pose next to it till Uncle Roscoe stepped out of his car. "Why looky there!" he cried. "It's little lady Delia." He smelled of cough drops, the bitter kind. She had thought she retained no mental picture of Uncle Roscoe, and she was startled to find him bobbing up like this, shifting his veiny leather Gladstone bag to his other hand so he could clamp her shoulder as they proceeded toward the house...
>
> "I was singing my doll a lullaby," she had told him in a confiding tone.
>
> She had always been such a *false* child, so eager to conform to the grown-ups' views of her.
>
> *Moon Above Wyndham Moor* was a disappointment. It just didn't seem very believable, somehow.

Observe how Tyler brings us back to the romance novel, the object that anchors us in the present as the scene begins.

Using "She remembered," as Tyler does here, or other versions of the same phrase, such as, "I recalled," or "He thought back to the time when" are just fine as a way to enter a flashback. It can be even more effective to use past perfect to slip effortlessly into a loop. Watch how Oakley Hall accomplishes this in this passage from his novel *Separations*.

Established already is that Mary is looking through her window at the San Francisco Bay. It is night. Her young friend, Nevada, is with her in the room. Nevada's face, reflected in this window, reminds Mary of her sister Esther, who disappeared when as young girls they were crossing the plains. Twelve-year-old Nevada demands the story. Mary tells her:

> "We'd seen no hostile Indians. The Yumans were very friendly, though they were great thieves."
> She closed her eyes. Nevada nudged her. "What *happened*?"
> "Esther and I slept under the wagon when it was hot. It was a moonlit night. Esther simply disappeared. Afterward it was thought that she may have gone out to relieve herself. And was taken."
> She had seen her sister rise in her white nightgown and slip out into the moonlight where the shadows were hard and sharp as sheet iron. Esther had picked her way toward the hillock with its cluster of standing rocks, disappearing among them. Mary had heard her cry out as she lay panting and terrified in her blankets. She had done nothing, had sounded no alarm, had suffered sleeplessly through the rest of the

night, and in the morning when Esther was discovered missing, had professed ignorance. *Why had she done nothing?* It was as though she had been paralyzed.

A string of tiny lights gleamed on the Oakland shore past the black bulk of Goat Island. The lights were blurred. She must not let herself dissolve into tears before her young friend.

As he slips us into the memory, Hall effectively avoids using the phrase, "*She remembered* that she had seen her sister..." The loop is short, and he uses the past perfect tense often. We are returned to the present by observing what Mary sees out her window—the activity established before we "looped." At the same time we are shown, rather than told, that she has tears in her eyes. As readers, we never lose track of where we are in time, although for almost three pages Hall moves among further details as well as Mary's emotions about this memory and what she actually says to young Nevada. His deft use of the past tense and the past perfect tense helps to make these transitions clear.

Bear in mind that a loop needs to further our understanding about an issue raised in and by the scene out of which it arises, and/or in your story as a whole.

We establish an activity for our character. This or another sensory cue moves her into the memory or thought process we wish to show the reader. As we emerge from this gap in the present tense of the story, we find that the activity we established has continued. The reader has been taken on a loop of memory and reflection. Without the confusion of time and space that flashbacks can engender, the reader returns to the ongoing scene richer in the knowledge of a character's history and motivations.

PUT IT TO WORK

EXERCISES:

14.   The Loop (page 245)

WHEN THE NARRATOR IS CLOSE

Point of view is the location in space from which the events of a story are perceived. Usually this point in space is a perspective called the narrator.

Perhaps because my background is in the dramatic and cinematic arts, an early way of understanding Point of View was to liken it to a moving camera. Although ultimately a limited analogy, the idea of a camera is a useful way to access this essential factor in the craft of a writer. It's a pretty sophisticated camera, capable of recording a great deal more than visuals and a soundtrack. In this analogy, when it is the eyes, as well as the nose, ears, tongue, and thoughts of a particular character, it perceives through *and only through* that character's senses.

This is particularly true of narrators that are "close" to the character they inhabit and describe: first and close third person. The *point of view character*, or the *narrator*, will hear, smell, taste, and feel—both physically and emotionally—the events of the story.

An author might begin writing her novel by using Margie as a first-person narrator, only to realize that the story is in fact Jim's (that is, he is the one who changes most, or he is the one to whom most of the story "happens"), and might be better served if told through his perspective. Sometimes such a decision solves problems of plot and motivation and even action that seemed irresolvable.

Similarly, our author might begin by writing the story in third person from Margie's point of view, but realizes this is limiting. He might decide to *rotate* between Margie and Jim, using two close third-person narrators, so that both perspectives are represented; he has Margie relate one chapter or section, and Jim another, separating the perspectives with space breaks. And there are options such as sliding and omniscience, discussed in "When the Narrator Has Distance."

As my understanding and appreciation of point of view grows, another image has become useful. It incorporates the word "persona," the poet's word for the narrator of a poem. *Persona* comes from the Latin, and ultimately, it is thought, from an Etruscan word for "mask." This is a useful image, for when we write we often don a sort of mask, a filter that is capable of changing not so much the faces but the voices of our narrators. It is mask used not so much as disguise but as alias, an identity. The analogy of a camera is largely a visual one, while the idea of a mask, or a filter, allows us to incorporate more subtle attributes of language. These language attributes are particularly useful in narrators who are close to a particular character—first and close third person—as they help us to create specific and distinct voices.

SENSORY PERCEPTIONS AND POINT OF VIEW

Sensory perceptions are essential tools in the creation of a specific point of view. They also come into play as we determine how far from or how close to a character we want our reader to be. In order of their capability to create proximity, these are:

→ Sight & Sound

→ Smell

→ Taste

→ Feeling (Tactile) &

→ Feelings (Emotional) & inner thought.

The perception of Sight is one that many people in a given scene share; unless one has eye problems, they will all probably see the same or similar things. Therefore, what a narrator sees may not necessarily give information about who is <u>doing</u> the seeing, unless it has been established that the narrator views from a particular place in the room or space. Or—and this is where the idea of "voice" comes in—the character's way of relating what he sees is odd, quirky, unique.

The perception of Sound is also common to all perspectives gathered in a single place; most of the characters will hear the tolling bell, the cat in heat, the snatch of conversation. Again, a narrator that records details of sound might not immediately reveal to the reader WHO is doing the perceiving. We can make the point of view clear by writing, "Tim heard the siren…" More effectively, we might show his reaction to what he hears, as in, "Tim sat up, heart pounding, as the wavering shrillness of the siren dopplered past."

Smell might be considered general: everyone in a room could smell garlic heated in olive oil, or someone's body odor—but would they? Much can be revealed by what someone smells, and how they think of that smell—or aroma—or stink. A great deal of nuance is attached to this sense: the scent of toasting bread, of Shalimar, of damp earth, may evoke one thing for one character and something quite different for another.

Smell, along with our next sensory impression, taste, are often attached to memories.

With Taste we begin to close in on the specific character doing the perceiving. Taste could be considered general; everyone at a table could report that "the roast beef is delicious." However, like the smell of a certain perfume, the taste of beef may arouse different responses in different characters. Above all, by the time we are close enough to a character to reveal what something tastes like, we are usually entering a specific point of view. Tim can't tell that Sarah's mouth is filled with the acrid taste of old coffee and sour milk. Actually, he could tell that, but then it would be <u>his</u> taste—and would communicate a great deal about the degree of intimacy between them.

Other than recording a character's inner monologue, Touch is the most specific way to locate point of view. When we describe what something feels like: silk against a bare arm, elastic too tight around a waist, the grit left in spinach against teeth, we are definitely in territory that only a specific individual can perceive: our point of view character. Tactile experience lets the reader know that we are all the way inside a narrator.

What a character <u>feels</u> is not limited to the tactile, of course, There is a reason emotions are known as "feelings," and as soon as a character feels anger, joy, confusion—in addition to heat, wet, chapped—we are "inside" the narrator. And of course, "He thought," or "She mused," and above all, reporting those thoughts and those musings, allows the reader to move in as close as close can be.

Proximity determines these choices. Depending on where a character is located dictates what he will see and hear. Charles, across the salon, cannot see the delicate silver work on the miniature box that Rose picks up off the table. Nor could Charles be aware of the piece of whispered conversation from a nearby loveseat that Rose, examining the box, inadvertently overhears. Nor, of course, could he feel the piece of filigree that she happens to press and that opens up a false bottom, where lies the scribbled note she palms and then pockets (a movement that perhaps he does see)... As we close in on or establish our point of view these sensory perceptions take on new significance.

Different characters notice different things about the same event, the same person. What, as well as how, a character notices helps reveal character—a specific point of view. By employing not only sensory perceptions and detail, but also syntax, vocabulary, even punctuation, we create how a character sees—and reports on what he sees.

CLOSE NARRATORS
& A MATTER OF VOICE

FIRST PERSON

First-person point of view can lend a marvelous immediacy and intimacy to the tone of the writing. Using a first-person narrator allows the author to easily access a character's inner thoughts, and places the reader in close proximity to the person to whom the experiences of the story are happening. First person is also used for "unreliable" narrators, those keeping something from the reader. (Although it could be argued that all "close" narrators are to some degree unreliable: If the writer is doing her job well, we are seeing the world only through that narrator's eyes, and the reader must do his own work in ascertaining the "truth" of that perspective.)

Henry James famously described first-person point of view as, "that accurst autobiographic form which puts a premium on the loose, the improvised, the cheap and the easy." While this may seem extreme, an author using a first-person narrator does have to guard against becoming too comfortable. It is easy to add detail that isn't vital to the narrative, and to be lazy with syntax while relying on a clever or engaging voice. If you are writing from fact—from what actually happened—first person can make it harder to distance yourself from the material, to fictionalize or "render" your material.

In addition, first person can create an almost claustrophobic proximity to your narrator. There is no way to tell the story except through what that character sees, using scenes in which she must be involved. (You can always rotate narrators of course, and utilize other points of view, but here I am addressing the story that is sustained by a single voice.) The author must find effective ways to reveal the character and even appearance of the narrator to the reader, layering in this understanding not by telling, through inner thought, but through action and through dialogue, through what she observes, and how she behaves.

But first person can be enormously engaging. Among its strengths is a strong and unique voice. An author's skillful use of syntax, grammar, and idiom, including colloquial word choice, lets the reader know these characters from the first sentence. Combining specific sensory perceptions with syntax and vocabulary, creates a powerful voice.

You don't know about me without you have read a book by the name of *The Adventures of Tom Sawyer*; but that ain't no matter. That book was made by Mr. Mark Twain, and he told the truth, mainly. There was things which he stretched, but mainly he told the truth.

In the very first lines of *The Adventures of Huckleberry Finn*, Mark Twain gives us an immediate sense of this brash, likable, and uneducated narrator. He also establishes that Huck cares about the truth, an issue that is reinforced and underscored in the story, when Huck realizes that he would rather go to hell than turn in Jim, the runaway slave.

> If you really want to hear about it, the first thing you'll probably want to know is where I was born, and what my lousy childhood was like and how my parents were occupied and all before they had me, and all that David Copperfield kind of crap, but I don't feel like going into it, if you want to know the truth. In the first place, that stuff bores me, and in the second place, my parents would have about two hemorrhages apiece if I told anything pretty personal about them. They're quite touchy about anything like that, especially my father. They're *nice* and all—I'm not saying that—but they're also touchy as hell.

This voice, Holden Caulfield's, from J.D. Salinger's *The Catcher in the Rye*, is full of energy It's driving the narrative; it has something <u>it needs to say</u>. It also doesn't give a hoot for grammar and syntax (try reading that first sentence aloud on one breath), and he'll swear if he wants to. He's educated, and probably attends a pretty good school—that *David Copperfield* reference. And the parents no doubt play a role in his life and in this narrative.

Holden is a persona, a mask, donned by Salinger to tell this story; Salinger has selected particular syntax (run-on sentences, and those famous italics) and detail with the purpose of creating Holden's voice, and, in the process, his character. Observe the persona Shirley Jackson adopts, also putting sentence structure, vocabulary, and selected details to work, as she creates Merricat Blackwood in *We Have Always Lived in the Castle*:

> My name is Mary Katherine Black-wood. I am eighteen years old, and I live with my sister Constance. I have often thought that with any luck at all I could have been born a werewolf, because the two middle fingers on both my hands are the same length, but I have had to be content with what I had. I dislike washing myself, and dogs, and noise. I like my sister Constance, and Richard Plantagenet, and *Amanita phalloides*, the death-cup mushroom. Everyone else in my family is dead.

Mary Katherine Blackwood is a very precise young woman. She likes lists. She likes order. She also likes odd and distinctly un-orderly things such as werewolves and the death-cup mushroom. She uses the same unadorned and unemotional language to inform us that most of her family is dead, a most intriguing invitation to read on. Rather different is the narrator from Toni Cade Bambara's story, "The Lesson":

> Back in the days when everyone was old and stupid or young and foolish and me and Sugar were the only ones just right, this lady moved on our block with nappy hair and proper speech and no makeup. And quite naturally we laughed at her, laughed the way we did at the junk man who went about his

business like he was some big-time president
and his sorry-ass horse his secretary. And we
kinda hated her too, hated the way we did
the winos who cluttered up our parks and
pissed on our handball walls and stank up
our hallways and stairs so you couldn't play
hide-and-seek without a goddamn gas mask.
Miss Moore was her name. The only woman
on the block with no first name. And she was
black as hell, cept for her feet, which were
fish white and spooky.

Here, too, the author skillfully employs syntax and
detail to let us know the world and the perspective of this
narrator. We know this takes place in another time (the
junk man with a horse) and in low-income housing (those
stinking hallways and stairs); that the narrator is either not
educated or is purposefully choosing an idiom true to this
world. Also clear is that Miss Moore commands a reluctant
respect, out of which the lesson of the title will no doubt
come.

It seems increasingly likely that I
really will undertake the expedition that has
been preoccupying my imagination now for
some days. An expedition, I should say,
which I will undertake alone, in the comfort
of Mr. Farraday's Ford; an expedition which,
as I foresee it, will take me through much of
the finest countryside of England... The idea
of such a journey came about, I should point
out, from a most kind suggestion put to me
by Mr. Farraday himself one afternoon almost a fortnight ago, when I had been dusting the portraits in the library. In fact, as I

recall, I was up on the step-ladder dusting the portrait of Viscount Wetherby...."

This is our introduction to Stevens, the butler-narrator of Kazuo Ishiguro's *Remains of the Day*: Right away, Stevens is revealed as someone who is diffident about stating his opinion, no doubt a necessary quality in a "good" butler, which Stevens prides himself on being. His vocabulary is self-important; he's fond of excess verbiage. He also thinks in semi-colons, a punctuation choice that helps establish the complicated workings of his mind. The curves and removes of this voice reflect Stevens's emotional distance from the story he is telling: "It seems increasingly likely," "as I foresee it," "I should point out," even as Ishiguro begins to place him in an environment (library), performing an action (dusting portraits) appropriate to his role. The qualities that make him a good butler contribute to the tragedy of this character; he chooses to stay oblivious to the feelings of others, even to the workings of his own heart. All of this is shown not only through the novel's action, but through the narrator's voice as well.

And back to our quarreling Margie and Jim:

I slammed the car door on whatever answer Jim might be dreaming up and for good measure told the closed window to shut up. Halfway across the parking lot I looked back, but Jim just sat there, staring ahead like he was driving someplace where the road was good and straight.

Pushing through the door of the diner was like walking into an enormous refrigerator that happened to have whirling fans and lots of tables and a ton of gabbing people in it. Signs on the walls shouted, *Meatloaf! Liver*

'n' Onions! Try Our Pie! A trucker leered
from the counter, a wedge of pancake drip-
ping syrup onto his thigh, taking in my cut-
offs. So they're short. I misjudged with the
first snip of scissors and then was commit-
ted. Like he's never made a mistake in his
life?

THIRD PERSON, CLOSE

The same attributes that create a strong first-person
narrator can be employed to create close third, a point of
view in which voice can also be effectively utilized. And
although the same problems that can dog first person
might manifest in close third—the need to be only "with"
that particular narrator, to see only what he sees, as he sees
it—some distance from the narrator is available. Although a
switch from first to close third might seem to resolve some
problems, such a solution is emphatically not simply a
matter of changing the pronoun from "I" to "she" or "he."
The way in which observations of the narrator are delivered
to the reader need to subtly and in some cases hugely shift.
Voice is created differently; for example, colloquial language, slang, which sounds appropriate in first, can sound
odd in third. See what happens if Holden talks to the
reader in third person:

If they really wanted to hear about it,
the first thing they'd probably want to know
is where he was born, and what his lousy
childhood was like and how his parents were
occupied and all before they had him, and all
that David Copperfield kind of crap, but he
doesn't feel like going into it, if they wanted
to know the truth.

Using so much colloquial language is unusual for a third-person narrator, and would be hard to sustain over a whole story or novel. In addition, the use of "they" instead of "you" and "he" instead of "I" allows—or forces—more distance between the reader and the narrator. We understand, subconsciously, that we're not hearing directly about an experience, but one that happened to someone the narrator "knows." This is true even when, as is the case in close third, the narrator is indistinguishable from the character to whom the experience is happening.

In close third, the camera is ever-present, over the character's shoulder, peering into the character's mind, narrating little more than what that one character happens to perceive. An acquaintance calls this "faux-first," but I don't agree. There are reasons for choosing third person other than simply not choosing first. As a writer you can use a little more distance and often the voice is not as "quirky" or unique or distinct. That doesn't make the writing or the point-of-view character any less effective; it's simply a choice the author makes.

In general, when we are ensconced with a close third-person narrator, it is jarring for the perspective to wander out and tell the reader what the character looks like. We need to obey the same strictures that first person imposes: we stay inside the narrator, seeing, hearing, perceiving only what she can see and hear and smell—perceive. We also need to avoid mirrors, reflections in windows, and the like to accomplish the task of revealing that a character is tall, or handsome, the color of her hair, or that she has a crooked nose. We can use what another character says, what the main character dislikes about herself, or comparisons to other, clearly-described characters, to reveal these details. This is where sensory perceptions— what and how a character notices—become enormously important. These details help build the scene, they also help reveal the character—the narrator—who is doing the observing.

> She'd missed it, Phoebe knew by the silence. Crossing the lush, foggy park, she heard nothing but the drip of condensation running from ferns and palm leaves. By the time she reached the field, its vast emptiness came as no surprise.
>
> The grass was a brilliant, jarring green. Debris covered it, straws, crushed cigarettes, a few sodden blankets abandoned to the mud.
>
> Phoebe shoved her hands in her pockets and crossed the grass, stepping over patches of bare mud. A ring of trees encircled the field, coastal trees, wind-bent and gnarled yet still symmetrical, like figures straining to balance heavy trays.

This is our introduction to Phoebe, from Jennifer Egan's *The Invisible Circus*. We sense right away that Phoebe has missed something more than the concert she came to attend: the details of the field bring to mind Woodstock, and we will soon discover that her sister, Faith, was part of that 60s world, a time Phoebe wishes she had known. (Her name translates as "pure," or "bright"; she is looking, literally and figuratively, for Faith.) The simile of the trees lets us know that Phoebe's work involves balancing heavy trays and she is, indeed, a waitress. There is an immediate tone of melancholy, appropriate to the narrator to whom we are being introduced.

Third person allows the author some distance, and allows the narrator distance from her or himself as well. An awkward self-consciousness develops, and the narrator isn't quite as appealing, if we hear from Phoebe in First Person:

> I'd missed it, I knew by the silence.
> Crossing the lush, foggy park, I heard noth-
> ing but the drip of condensation running
> from ferns and palm leaves. By the time I
> reached the field, its vast emptiness came as
> no surprise.

A very different tone emanates from Dupree, in
Stephen Cooper's story, "The Paper Man":

> Dupree's last cast was perfect. The
> hand-tied fly seemed to hang in the twilight
> for a long and brilliant second before floating
> down to kiss the surface of the water. He had
> finally hit the smallest ring at the pool's far
> end. If only he could cast like that up on the
> river, where presentation really counted, in-
> stead of here, in his freshly chlorinated
> swimming pool. Still, it was one way to end a
> vacation, better than some he could imagine.
> He reeled in the line, propped his rod against
> the patio bar and picked up the flexible bottle
> of charcoal lighter fluid; he was about to
> douse the stacked briquets when Jennifer
> called from the kitchen window...

We understand that appearance counts to Dupree;
the way Cooper has constructed the first few sentences
allows us to think that Dupree is casting into a river. We are
surprised—it's the first of several lies that the narrator
reveals to himself, and to the reader—to find he's casting
into a swimming pool, and a freshly chlorinated one at that.
In fact, the details gradually accrue to reflect the sanitized,
suburban, ultimately empty life this "paper man" inhabits,
and that the events of the story will cause him to confront.

In addition to penning a most wonderful first sentence, Rhoda Huffy manages to reveal a lot about her narrator in this opening to her novel, *The Hallelujah Side*:

> It had been a Second Coming sky all day, which meant they might be in heaven by this evening. Roxanne stood by the mirror trying to make spit curls. Stupidly, her red hair hung there, causing her to glare out at her sister, Colleen the beautiful. Roxanne dropped the spit curl (which went straight), turned to the piano, and hit high C. Then she walked her fingers on the white keys, five notes up the scale and four notes down. Each rang. Over on the couch, Roxanne's mother, Zelda Fish, sneezed again, especially hard this time. Sister Fish had the flu, but if they went up she would be cured instantly. Roxanne picked up her doll, Miss Jennifer Smith, and walked back and forth across the living room, back and forth, ready to go. It would happen in the twinkling of an eye, the dead rising first, then the saints going up to meet Him in the air, no time to get your belongings.
>
> "Shhhh," said Roxanne to the doll ear.

Huffy has painted Roxanne as interested in both spit curls and her doll, which neatly shows her straddling the abyss between girl- and woman-hood. She thinks of her own mother as "Sister Fish"; religiosity plays a huge role in her life, as does or will music. Although the Second Coming will happen quickly, with no time to fetch belongings, she's got hold of her doll, just in case.

For another example of a third-person close narrator, review pages 82-85, an excerpt from and discussion of Anne Tyler's *Ladder of Years*.

A shift in tone—sometimes a large shift—occurs when an author purposefully plays with Point of View. If you give this a try you will see that a character will actually talk, behave, and think quite differently depending upon whether he or she is written in first person, close third, or in the more distant perspectives discussed in "When the Narrator has Distance." For instance, I found it most surprising to see how spunky Margie was when I wrote that bit in first person—in third she seemed far more mousy and "put-upon." Experimenting with these possibilities may help establish what you do and do not want to do with your point of view. It will also give interesting insights into the opinions and history and the personality of a given character.

Close narrators are not limited to first and third: A second-person point of view narrates Jay McKinerney's *Bright Lights, Big City*, and forces an intimacy (you are he) on the reader: "You are not the kind of guy who would be at a place like this at this time of the morning. But here you are, and you cannot say that the terrain is entirely unfamiliar…"

Alice Sebold in the lovely *The Lovely Bones* creates a first-person <u>omniscient</u> narrator, to whom we are as close as is possible, considering that she is talking to us from heaven.

First person plural is used by William Faulkner in "A Rose for Emily": "When Miss Emily Grierson died, our whole town went to her funeral," the story begins, and we gradually understand that the town is the point of view on the events.

ROTATING NARRATORS

Rotating your narrators is a useful way to look through two or more characters' eyes and can be done with third as well as with first-person narrators.

> Jim waited until Margie had disappeared behind the diner's glass doors, then hauled himself out of the car, blinking against the sun that bounced off the windows and the chrome and the paint jobs of the cars surrounding his. He shook his head. The bottoms of Margie's butt-cheeks showed in those cutoffs of hers. Not that she could hear a whit of criticism, not without sparking. He crouched on the pavement beside the open door and felt around beneath his seat for his sunglasses, where they'd fallen when he yanked them off for Margie's *comfort* during the charming chat they'd just enjoyed, which actually meant sitting still and enduring one of her rants. He used his t-shirt to clean them up a bit and, as he slid them into the little notch on his nose that seemed to exist just for that purpose, felt immediately better.

When a writer rotates narrators, the changes in point of view happen at specific and natural points—a space break, a chapter break. That is, the rotation happens at organic stopping places in the narrative, not, as happens when the narration slides from character to character, within a scene or even within a paragraph. (See "When the Narrator has Distance.") Some writers put the name of the character above the section devoted to that point of view. Other writers make the change clear by immediately establishing the new character in some activity or in dialogue, letting the reader know through whose eyes we are going to be looking during this section of the story.

The choice to rotate points of view is an effective way to tell a story when the author wants to stay fairly close to his characters and sees no need to employ the more demanding and encompassing perspective of an omniscient narrator. To be effective, it's best to establish a limited number of narrators.

Max Byrd begins his novel *Grant* with some perspectives on the president of that name; as Chapter Two begins, we meet Nicholas Trist, one of the novel's several narrators:

> "An author," said Maudie Cameron, aged ten, wearing a crisp white pinafore and an expression of pug-nosed disdain, "is a dreadful person who writes books."
>
> Nicholas Trist III scratched his chin stubble with the palm of his hand and studied a crystal decanter of amber-brown whiskey just to the child's left, on a tabletop otherwise uselessly cluttered with little colored porcelain figures of cats and dogs in bonnets.
>
> "My father never reads books," Maudie said. "He says books are a damn-blasted waste of time."
>
> "That's quite enough, Maudie." The child's governess was knitting or sewing or vivisecting something furry and blue in her lap, and without actually looking up she narrowed her eyes in a professional frown. Trist caught a glimpse of his own red-rimmed eyes in one of the room's six mirrors. He placed his hand on his knee and stood up and dropped his hat.
>
> "*You* wrote a book," Maudie said.

"But nobody read it," Trist assured her.

The reader has been in Trist's point of view for only a few paragraphs, learning things that characterize him—he scratches his chin stubble, he studies a decanter of whiskey—but it is that telling adverb, "uselessly" (describing those cats and dogs in bonnets), that begins to pull us into his actual perceptions; the verb "vivisect" lands us firmly inside his mind. We feel suddenly intimate; it's as if Trist has just thrown us a quirky look, a raised eyebrow, which lets us in on a joke we share. When I read this section aloud there is almost always laughter at those two places, an indication that the author has successfully engaged the reader in Trist. We begin to know this narrator: we suspect Trist has a sense of humor; he has had experience with vivisecting, or at least with blood and guts; he has a slightly morbid tendency; he is fond of whiskey. And as the book unfolds these characteristics prove to be true. Trist's voice—and the reader's trust in that voice—have been established.

"The most public goddam banquet of the century was scheduled to be a Grand Old Army reunion..." Chapter Three of this same novel begins, and as briefly as we've been with Trist, we know this is not his voice. We soon discover that we re now in the jaundiced perspective of the newspaperman Cadwallader; the "goddam" immediately establishes this new and very different narrator of the novel.

There are countless other examples of rotating points of view: *Crazy in Alabama*, by Mark Childress; *The Robber Bride*, by Margaret Atwood; I employ the technique in *Catching Heaven*. In *The Poisonwood Bible* Barbara Kingsolver rotates the sisters' idiosyncratic first-person voices. Jane Hamilton, in *A Map of the World*, rotates two first-person narrators: we hear from the wife, then the husband, then return to the wife.

When a writer begins to grapple with and understand the options and thematic concerns that can be expressed <u>through</u> and <u>with</u> point of view, many possibilities emerge. In "For Esmé with Love and Squalor," for instance, J.D. Salinger dramatizes how distant a narrator has become from himself as a result of his war experiences: the first half of the story is told in first person; the same narrator tells the second half of the story in third. William Faulkner doesn't rotate but presents the first person perspectives of three very different brothers in *The Sound and the Fury*, a technique that Julia Glass employs in *Three Junes*: presenting three narrators who don't know they know each other, part of the novel's charm.

IN CONCLUSION

A writer reveals and a reader discovers truths about a character through specific language, as Huck's "without you have read" and Cadwallader's "goddam," and Merricat's precise lists demonstrate. Trist's perception that the governess is "vivisecting" her knitting lets us see into his mind, as Stevens's repetitions, circumlocutions, and semi-colons allow us to see into his. In addition to sensory perceptions (what our characters notice, and what those perceptions show the reader about them), word choice, vocabulary, punctuation grammar, even sentence length and sentence structure allow us to create specific voices, which reveal to our readers the hearts and minds of our characters. If we could hear them speak, this is the way their voices might actually sound.

PUT IT TO WORK

EXERCISES:

It might also be useful to look at:

THIS POV STUFF

As we move into a discussion of more distant and perhaps more complex narrators, some writers ask, what's the big deal about this POV stuff?

"Why can't I just do it? If I want to move the point of view—even if I don't *know* I'm moving the point of view—who gives a hoot? John Grisham shifts the point of view *all the time*, and he's a *zillionaire*."

Students whose ambition it is to write romance novels tell me that there is an expectation in the genre, and from their editors, to slide the point of view around. Other genre novels—thrillers, crime novels, mysteries, numerous bestsellers—seem to pay little or no attention to these niceties. Bottom line, some writers seem to wonder: *who cares*, as long as the story gets told?

Well, it's true that a lot of readers don't care. So I suppose our point of view decisions are at least in part decided by the audience for which we are writing. And frankly, I happily— delightedly—let go of all my tidy little rules when a writer comes along, grabs me by the hand (and throat and mind), and plunges me into a story, leaping and skittering from character to character as the story unfolds. Larry McMurtry's *Lonesome Dove* is a brilliant example of this. Diane Johnson's *Le Divorce* is another. And these writers aren't laboring over what they're doing with every sentence, every shift in perspective. They're just plunging through the surf of their story, getting it told, and having (it's clear) a fine time in the process.

During my first year at the Iowa Writers' Workshop I trekked across the broad swiftly-flowing Iowa River and downstream along its banks to the Music Department to take a music history course. One of the many things that stuck with me as a result of those two semesters immersed in another art form is the knowledge that in art as in life the pendulum will always swing. After staggering through the lush, ecstatic tropical forests of the Romantics, we moved to the minimal, ascetic (and acerbic) anti-emotionalism of the Twelve Tone composers: arbitrary selections of a limited notational palette, with little or no sense of traditional tonality.

In the literary arts, the swing from Romance manifested in other ways: the Noble Savage morphed to the Individual Being; the (Distant) Goodness of God to the (Benign) Indifference of the Universe. In addition, the twentieth century's obsession with psychology brought with it a common understanding of mental processes, how traumas affect character and behavior—perspectives and methods reflected in literature. Having a Big Narrator tell us what is driving a character, what is making him tick, became less appealing; readers wanted to see, to discover, for themselves.

But this at-times claustrophobic proximity (one writer has compared it to having one's face pressed up against a cinema screen) is undergoing its own pendulum swing; writers—and readers—are interested again in the Bigger Picture, in gaining some distance. Maybe this has something to do with the rise of fundamentalism (another pendulum swing): either a need for or a rediscovery of god and religion and even meaning that may have been abandoned for a while in the wake of the Existentialists. People want that Big Eye. They want to be Told. They want the larger world, the connected and meaningful society, that perhaps such a perspective implies.

But I am too aware as a reader (because I school myself to be aware as a writer) not to be bothered when such a point of view doesn't work: when I am jarred by something, when I am pushed out of what John Gardner calls the "vivid and continuous fictional dream." This jarring can take place when a detail is incorrect. And it can take place when, for example, I've been in one point of view and suddenly, inexplicably, that character knows the name of a character he has not yet met. Sometimes this can work— and I hope this next essay will reveal why I think so—but usually it makes me mistrust the "authority" telling the story.

A lot of novels, many of them genre novels, do slide and move and jump the point of view and these books are read avidly—we see that as we lug our over-the-shoulder bags down the aisle of a loaded plane. I think it's above all because these readers like the sense of a Big Narrator. They like the idea—especially for a plane ride, or as a way to utterly escape the humdrum or even tragic details of life— that for this brief time they can dispense with subjectivity and luxuriate in a narrator with bigger fish to fry. A narrator that knows more and can and will go anywhere, rather than one that sticks close to a single character or two (although these books can be—and of course this is the reason we read them—like hanging out with an intriguing new friend).

If you're reading this essay—if you're interested in this POV stuff—it's because you sense that there is something missing from how you're employing these larger perspectives, or because you have an ambition to employ them. And you are reading this with an expectation, a desire, to use point of view with purpose.

That's probably the biggest word I find I employ, the longer I tangle with trying to be the most effective writer I can be, and work to help others towards that same goal: Purpose. To do what we are doing with purpose. I haven't been able to ask Mr. Grisham over a glass of beer if he jumps the point of view in, say, a courtroom scene, with purpose, or if it's because his excellent storytelling mind just knows it's the right thing and the right time to do that. It's a "style thing," and one of the great satisfactions of writing is that we begin to discover what our style is. And it might be about shifting points of view in the middle of a sentence. And it might be discovering that employing an omniscient voice is what you were born to do.

WHEN THE NARRATOR HAS DISTANCE

With a first-person narrator, such as Mark Twain's Huckleberry, and a close third-person narrator, such as Jennifer Egan's Phoebe, the point of view stays close to a single character for the entire novel. This sense of proximity is also true of rotating narrators. In his novel, *Cold Mountain*, Charles Frazier uses syntax, vocabulary, and figures of speech to differentiate between one of his narrators, Inman, and the other, Ada. Frazier is not the narrator; he is the author, creating the two characters that narrate their sections of the novel.

This separation between author and narrator remains fairly clear in first- and close third-person points of view. When a writer uses a distant point of view, however, this sense of separation often blurs—is blurred with purpose. At times a writer chooses not to separate himself from his narrator, as when Henry James writes, in an early passage of *The Portrait of a Lady*, "Those that I have in mind in beginning to unfold this simple history…" James is not a participant in the action; he is the author-as-narrator, relating events. In a more modern example, John Fowles, in *The French Lieutenant's Woman*, clearly delights in "intruding" himself on the story he is creating; for example, after keeping us enraptured, if troubled, by a chapter that seems to be drawing elements of the plot to a sudden close, he writes, "And now, having brought this fiction to a thoroughly traditional ending, I had better explain that although all I have described in the last two chapters happened, it did not happen in the way you may have been led to believe…"

In general, however, the author and his or her narrator are discrete entities. The author develops the person telling the story just as he creates the characters, the plot and his themes. Distant perspectives don't always have a "voice," as a first-person narrator often has (although sometimes they definitely do); nor do they necessarily allow the reader to feel as intimate with the narrator as, say close third person does.

These more distant points of view include Distant, Sliding, and of course Omniscient narrators. The differences among these points of view can at first seem confusing, or even arbitrary. Each of them seems to entail a narrator with a larger perspective—one that knows more—than any single character in the story. But there are differences—and they seem to boil down to degrees of distance.

John Gardner, in his essential discussion of these ideas in *The Art of Fiction*, has precisely named it <u>psychic distance</u>: "the distance the reader feels between himself and the events in the story."

THE DISTANCE A READER FEELS

Point of View: The location of the narrator viewing and relating the events of the story. The narrator is situated in relation to those events; the narrator is also situated in relation to the reader.

A writer can purposefully move that view. For instance, we can move an omniscient narrator closer to the action, analogous to a movie's "slow zoom," and diminish the distance between that which is doing the viewing and that which is being viewed. And the reader is along for that ride.

Ideally, the writer keeps the reader abreast of such movement, the narrowing of the distance, and doesn't jump too close too quickly:

> In the late 1800's, before the Far West was settled, a young man and his bride finished loading supplies into a covered wagon. Damn. What a purty thing his gal was. He'd just finish heave-hoing these sacks of flour, 'n' then hit the trail.

This shift in voice from that of a far-off narrator to close-in inner monologue might well baffle, as well as amuse, most readers, as would a sudden jump from the far-off visual to the close-in tactile:

> The sun worked its way up and over a pair of low-slung hills, its light flowing across the green fields of Walter Cathcart, who felt his heart pumping from the exertion of hefting those damn flour sacks in the wagon.

The degree of distance the author selects establishes where the narrator is in relation to what he or she or it is describing.

The degree of intimacy the author gives the point of view helps characterize the narrator.

Through selection of vocabulary, syntax, imagery, as well as strategic use of sensory perceptions, emotion, and inner thought, the author creates a narrator—and in the process, a character. These ideas are introduced in "When the Narrator is Close"; here is a more-thorough discussion of the concept.

SENSORY PERCEPTIONS, PROXIMITY, & POINT OF VIEW

SIGHT:

What can be <u>seen</u> does not necessarily place the reader in the eyes and shoes of a particular narrator.

> The man stood at a podium at the front of the room, reading aloud from the pile of papers before him.

We aren't yet sure where the point of view is, nor do we have a sense of who is doing the looking. Even adding a little more detail regarding sound won't clarify the point of view—if <u>who</u> is doing the seeing and hearing is not clear.

SOUND:

> Wearing his usual three-piece charcoal-gray suit, Walter Tilden stood at a podium at the front of the room and read in a monotone from a pile of paper.

Naming the man might make us wonder if Mr. Tilden is the point of view. However, since so far we still have only <u>sight</u> and <u>sound</u>, neither very specific nor vividly drawn, we still aren't sure who is doing the looking, where the <u>point</u> or location of the view is. And would Tilden think of his own delivery as a "monotone?" (If we find out that he does, it will reveal something about his attitude towards himself and his life.)

> Walter Tilden stood at a podium at the front of the room, and read in a monotone from a pile of paper. Frank took notes, as he'd been instructed to do.

So is the point of view Frank? Even now we aren't sure where the narrator is located; the writer hasn't necessarily made it clear. Is Frank watching Mr. Tilden? Mr. Tilden, Frank? Is there another character altogether, who is watching both?

What happens if another sense is incorporated?

SMELL:

> Walter Tilden stood at the podium at the front of the room and read in a monotone from a pile of paper. Frank took notes, as he'd been instructed to do. The aroma of stale coffee permeated the room...

We still aren't entirely sure where the point of view is. But what happens if we anchor that smell:

> Walter Tilden stood... Frank took notes... The smell of stale coffee permeated the room, and Stacy, sitting beside Frank, lifted her wrist to sniff the cologne she'd dabbed there that morning.

We seem to be moving into Stacy's point of view, but all of this is visual: this could still be an "outside," or distant narrator recording the events taking place at this lecture.

> Walter Tilden stood... Frank took notes.... The smell of stale coffee permeated the room, and Stacy, sitting beside Frank, lifted her wrist to sniff the lemony cologne she'd dabbed there that morning.

The adjective "lemony" moves us closer to Stacy's point of view; presumably that is her description. If we were to use an adverb like "gratefully" (as in, "she sniffed gratefully"), we'd become ensconced there; "grateful" is Stacy's emotion toward the aroma, her thought regarding it. But "gratefully" is an adverb, and while adverbs have their place, there are additional and more effective ways to establish proximity to a narrator.

TASTE:

> The smell of stale coffee permeated the room, and Stacy, sitting beside Frank, lifted her wrist to sniff the lemony cologne she'd dabbed there that morning. The remains of a latte she'd finished two hours ago still coated her tongue, a rubbery sheath of sour milk.

There is no way Frank can know how the coffee on Stacy's tongue <u>tastes</u>—or, even more to the point—<u>feels</u>. These two sensory perceptions move us very close to a specific point of view.

FEELING: TACTILE

> As if the smell of stale coffee and Mr. Tilden's drone weren't enough to drive a woman crazy, she'd purchased size A pantyhose. Again. What made her think she'd ever return to her pert, gamine, petite former self? She pulled at the waistband. The angry red furrow the elastic was even now goring into her flesh would take over an hour—once she got home and peeled off the sausage casings that currently enveloped her legs—to disappear.

Here Stacy is <u>feeling</u> the waistband, and having thoughts about it as well; we are anchored in her perspective. We're also getting a sense of her voice, which, if we were to read on, strengthens her point of view:

FEELING: EMOTIONAL

> ...and peeled off the pantyhose-to disappear, but that didn't keep her from longing for the pastries piled on a plate beside the coffee urn, couldn't keep her from imagining the

cinnamon tucked into the crevices of one of those rolls, the globs of sugar, the crunchy walnut bits. Even with Frank in all his snotty, long-nosed disapproval beside her she would lick her fingers to get every crumb, and then she would feel good and guilty about the whole thing and life would be even worse than it already was. She sighed, and slumped in her seat, then sat bolt upright as Frank hissed, "Stacy! Stop fussing!"

A character's emotional response and inner thought are last and closest in this series of "proximities," bringing us most intimately to the person doing the viewing. In addition, the author is presumably selecting these details to give us a sense of Stacy, in this case of her unappeased appetites and sense of inferiority, things that the reader assumes are important to the story as it unfolds.

Thought, or inner monologue, can be just another way of telling rather than doing the hard work of showing, but used judiciously is useful:

THOUGHT:

Stacy sighed and slumped, and Frank shot her a glance, irritation like half-chewed peanuts in his throat. "Stacy! Stop fussing!" He wanted to poke her. That twitching, never still, always up and down, in and out, what he hated most about living with her, with Tilden's idiotic lecture hard enough to follow without her endless fidgets. And he was going to have to find something positive to say to the Boss when this endless day was over...

Proximity, intimacy, have a great deal to do with the sensory perception being utilized. Sight—depending on context of course—is perhaps the most "distant"; thoughts and feelings—tactile and above all emotional—the closest.

The point of view can slide pretty seamlessly if we utilize this understanding, moving from what Stacy might be feeling to an action of Frank's and thus to his thought. And we don't have to write "Frank thought," if an action or observation or feeling makes it clear who is doing the thinking. This is a matter of style, but often phrases such as "he wondered," or "she thought" are ancillary and even intrusive if the character doing the wondering and thinking has already been made clear.

A writer wants to establish the authority in a story or novel fairly early, including the point(s) of view she intends to use. Readers want to put their trust in the author: they want to know, however subliminally, that the point of view, like everything else in the story, is selected and is utilized with purpose. If there are shifts—from one character to another, or from, say, an aerial view to deep within a character's mind—there is confidence in where and how the narrator and by extension the author is taking them.

DIMINISHING DISTANCE; INCREASING PROXIMITY

Once we understand how to utilize sensory perception and detail, we can begin to control the movement from distance to proximity:

> In the late 1840s, Walter Cathcart and his wife Emma left their farm in Illinois, setting out for the Far West and a new life.

Except for the date, this offers the reader few specifics.

In 1847, as spring began to announce itself in the hills and valleys of Illinois, Walter Cathcart loaded a last barrel of molasses into his wagon, and turned to his reluctant wife, Emma.

Spring "announcing itself" helps ground the reader somewhat, as does specifying the "barrel of molasses" and the adjective, "reluctant."

The sun crested the low-slung Illinois hills and lighted the top branches of the Cathcarts' apple trees, just breaking into flower. The light found its way down the trunks of trees, slanted across a road, slid across the yard and then up the white-washed wall of a farmhouse, where a wooden door creaked open, and Walter Cathcart snagged the heel of his boot around it to kick it all the way ajar. He muscled a barrel over the flagstones and across the dusty yard to the waiting wagon. Panting, he paused and looked up, a heavy-set, bearded man, and studied the woman who drooped against the picket fence. There were yellow blooms on one of her bushes already, and it was only April. "Emma," he said. "Emma, you set?"

Emma straightened, retied her bonnet strings, still studying her rose bushes. There was no way to bring them along. She turned, thin in thin gingham, shawl pulled across bony shoulders. "I guess."

In this case we get a great many more sensory perceptions, but they are mostly visuals—what the point of view can <u>see</u>. A reader could think we're in Walter's perspective, but the narrator tells us he's "heavy set," a detail that doesn't seem like something Walter himself would think. The phrase, "there was no way to bring them along," could be a thought of Emma's; or, if we were firmly lodged in Walter's point of view, might be his observation. But because we've yet to move into a specific perspective, we probably take it as a statement of fact by a more distant, perhaps omniscient, narrator.

> Walter Cathcart hefted the last of the sacks of flour into the wagon, wiped the back of his forearm across his brow, and flexed his muscles, which ached from the barrels and ploughs and benches he'd moved and lifted and lugged and shoved and cursed the last few days. But at last he was ready, at dawn they would finally leave.
>
> He didn't have to look for Emma. She was leaning against the picket fence he'd built for her when she first started that rose-ordering business. One was in bloom already, the Ophir, she called it, and its scent, coming at him on the breeze, was golden as its blooms. But there was no way to take it—no way to take any of them. No room, for one thing. And how would they survive months across lands with hardly water enough for the oxen? Although the look in her brown eyes when last night she pleaded for them made him feel an awful wretch. "Emma," he said, as gently as he knew how. "You set?"

As we move even closer and are given more tangible detail, we are also given a firmer sense of the point of view. Again, proximity plays a role: We can observe the sweat on Walter's brow and not necessarily feel "placed" in Walter's perspective. However, if we get an aroma (the roses), or especially a feeling (the aching muscles), or a thought ("at last he was ready," and, "no room, for one thing"), we've moved all the way in to Walter's "head"; we're firmly in his point of view.

When a point of view verbalizes too much inner thought, it has perhaps moved too close and has the potential to be (unintentionally) humorous.

> Damn. They'd been packin' for days. One more of these sacks of flour and they could get out. Arragh! Up onto the wagon it went. And there stood Emma, eyein' those roses of hers. Dang 'n' blast! Where in dickens did she think he was supposed to put 'em?
>
> "Emma!" No, no, good lord, man, talk kinder to her! There she went, wipin' her eyes with that apron o' hers, like she been doin' so much of these days. "Emma," he said again. "Come on, now. You leave them roses be."

With these ideas of distance and proximity, as well as an understanding of the role sensory perceptions play in creating a specific point of view, let's examine some narrators that have distance.

SLIDING NARRATORS

Some might argue that "sliding" or "distant" narrators are simply omniscient narrators. But for me, an omniscient narrator, to be truly "omniscient," needs to provide a perspective on the story that is larger than any single character's point of view. When the author or narrator of a novel doesn't give the reader a sense of a larger intelligence, when he simply moves "who is telling the story"

from character to character, I think of it as "sliding" the
narrator.

> Margie slammed the car door and
> leaned down to look through the window, but
> Jim's mulish, implacable profile did not
> move. She balled her hand into a fist and hit
> the glass. "And just in case you didn't hear
> me the first three times, SHUT UP." Her fist
> hurt, and she cradled it with her other hand
> as she headed across the parking lot towards
> the diner. The sun-baked asphalt billowed
> hot air up her legs.
>
> Jim finally turned his head to look af-
> ter her. Her legs were too skinny and too
> white sticking out of those cutoffs and her
> butt cheeks showed and it was time for her to
> wash her hair. It was lacking its usual
> bounce and shine, and the same could be
> said for her.
>
> He found his dark glasses, locked the
> car, and—in case she might be looking—
> slapped his cap nonchalantly against his
> thigh as he headed towards the doors
> through which she'd disappeared. He paused
> to see if the *LA Times* might be represented
> in the crowd of newspaper dispensers hud-
> dled outside the diner. Beyond the tinted
> glass that separated them he could make out
> Margie's silhouette. She bent one knee, then
> the other, lifted the hair off her neck, raised
> her face to the cool air drifting down from
> the fans overhead. A waitress raced by, a cof-
> feepot in each hand.

"Sit anywhere you like, Hon," Rosie called as she headed towards table 7. That was one skinny beanpole standing by the door. She could use a Grand Slam breakfast, by the look of her. Rosie smiled her cheeriest smile. "I'll be right with you."

As we've discussed, the point of view moves when a character thinks something ("her hair was lacking its usual bounce...," "That was one skinny beanpole") or feels something (the cool air from the fans). Unless it is employed with grace and precision this technique has drawbacks, but while depth of characterization may suffer when a writer slides the point of view around, it can be a convenient way to let the reader know something about several characters in a short space of time.

When a writer chooses to slide the point of view among various characters without a space-break or chapter-break, she should have good reason to do so—it should be done with and on purpose. As a teacher and editor, I find that early authors are often unaware that they are sliding or shifting their point of view. Or the writer has not yet determined from whose point of view the story should be told, and moves to the perspective that suits him for that moment. Or it's an awkward or limited use of a supposedly omniscient narrator. Even though the perspective slides, glides, leaps from one character to another, the reader does not necessarily get a feeling of a larger intelligence, an authority that knows more than any single character in the tale knows. The story is related through a series of perspectives, but the camera, or the form of the narration, never rises high enough to provide the reader with the sense of an over-arching intelligence. This may feel like hair-splitting, but in fact affects the tone and even theme of a story.

Sliding narrators can be useful (especially as practice for creating omniscience), but your readers may feel jerked around; they don't know though whose eyes they're supposed to be looking, whose "side" they're supposed to be on. And if the reader knows what several characters are thinking, the climax of a given scene can be drained of its excitement. Perhaps most importantly, by revealing the inner thoughts of several characters, the author may be relying on those thoughts to <u>tell</u> the content of the scene rather than doing the hard and important work of <u>showing</u> that content and even the scene's subtext.

However, in the hands of a skillful writer, the technique is most effective. Here's an excerpt from Jennifer Egan's *Look at Me*. Present at a table in a restaurant are a young girl named Charlotte, in whose point of view we've spent a lot of time; her parents, Harris and Ellen; and her eccentric Uncle Moose and his wife, Priscilla. As the point of view is passed around the table like a butter dish, observe how Egan uses emotions, opinions, and feelings to ground the point of view, however briefly:

> ...to Charlotte, her uncle's exile was more intriguing than that. At night, the house thick with sleep, she would peer out her bedroom window at the trees and sky and feel **(we are definitely with Charlotte here)** the presence of a mystery. Some possibility that included her—separate from her present life and without its limitations. A secret... She was an exile, too.
>
> The waitress arrived with a giant round tray, which she set on a stand near their table.
>
> "Char, go get Ricky, would you, honey?" Ellen asked.

The instant Charlotte was gone (**Charlotte leaves, but the point of view stays at the table**), Harris spoke urgently to Moose and Priscilla, though only Priscilla returned his gaze. (**"Returned his gaze" begins to move the POV to him; we see what he sees.**) "You could do me a hell of a favor," he said, "if you'd ask Charlotte why she's switching schools."

"She's leaving Baxter?" Priscilla said.

"We didn't find out until a few weeks ago. She says she's going to East." The idea made Harris frantic. (**We're now totally in his POV; he is made "frantic," and we get his thoughts regarding why.**) East was public, blue-collar, a bunch of machinists' kids! In general he marveled at his daughter's equanimity—the Lord, in His mystery, had apportioned his son the beauty and his daughter the strength. But at times he was overcome by an urge to break Charlotte, make her see how resolutely the deck was stacked in her disfavor. As if knowing this would protect her from something worse. Harris wanted to save her.

"Have you asked her why?" Priscilla said.

Harris flung up his hands. "Have I asked!"

"She's completely closed," Ellen said, "she won't talk to either one of us." She was craving a cigarette. (**We're now with Ellen; the "craving" anchors us in her POV.**) Lately she'd begun sneaking them at home: Kools, which made her feel like a teenager.

"Of course I'll try," Priscilla said, "but if she won't talk to you..."

Here's another example, from Myla Goldberg's *Bee Season*. Here the point of view does not slide so much as jump between Eliza and her brother Aaron. Goldberg keeps us anchored to emotions—Eliza <u>stifles</u> an urge, Aaron <u>realizes</u> and <u>wonders</u>, Eliza is <u>reminded</u> of one thing, and <u>likes</u> another—the reader is never in doubt about where the point of view, however temporarily, is lodged. Here, Eliza's seldom-satisfied and absent-minded father has mislaid, thinking it's unimportant, the letter that announces she's won a spelling bee.

> Saul, Aaron, and Eliza sort through the drifts of paper. It is Aaron who finds the envelope, smudged from Eliza's hands and taped where she had torn it.
> "Is this it?"
> For a split second Eliza pictures opening the envelope and finding nothing there **(here, of course we're clearly in Eliza's head)**, the letter having been absorbed into the dense piles of paper around it. She stifles the urge to snatch the envelope from her brother.
> Aaron realizes **(POV to Aaron)** that his standing mental image of Eliza is three years out of date; in his mind she is still a shy second grader quietly insistent upon matching her socks with her shirt every morning. He wonders when she started parting her hair on the left and if she's always had the nervous habit of sucking in her cheeks.
> The way Saul reaches for the envelope reminds Eliza **(back to Eliza)** of first-time To-

rah bearers, stiff-armed with their fear of mishandling the sacred burden. She likes that he uses a letter opener instead of his fingers. The smile that appears momentarily erases years of report card trauma.

"This," Saul says in a reverent voice, "is a beautiful thing.

DISTANT NARRATORS

Third-person point of view doesn't suddenly stop being close and become omniscient. There is a continuum, an arc like a gauge on a meter, with perhaps close third inner monologue at one end of the dial, and totally omniscient at the other. A "distant" point of view is a little over on the omniscient side of this continuum. Such a narrator stays outside a particular character, revealing to the reader not only insights that particular character might not have, but even that character's appearance—something it's difficult for a close third narrator to do. This separation of author and narrator may be employed simply as a way to begin a story—the narrator is not (yet) a particular character, but provides context and information that particular narrator might not know, or would not communicate in that way. Sometimes that distant voice will assert itself here and there throughout a given story—offering perspectives that might be rather more, or rather different than the point of view's perspective. This offers an author some separation to play with, when adhering too closely to a particular point of view feels limiting, even squashed. It's a way to let some breath in.

However, this is not quite the same as an omniscient point of view—it doesn't necessarily rise out to give us a larger perspective on the themes and story being revealed.

Joyce Carol Oates's story, "Where Are You Going, Where Have You Been," is a wonderful example of this. As the story begins, we are shown the narrator, Connie, from the outside, just as—and this is thematically part of Oates's point—she is herself outside, watching herself. She is in her own movie, the subject of her own pop song:

> Her name was Connie. She was fifteen and she had a quick nervous giggling habit of craning her neck to glance into mirrors, or checking other people's faces to make sure her own was all right. Her mother, who noticed everything and knew everything and who hadn't much reason any longer to look at her own face, always scolded Connie about it. "Stop gawking at yourself, who are you? You think you're so pretty?" she would say. Connie would raise her eyebrows at these familiar complaints and look right through her mother, into a shadowy vision of herself as she was right at that moment: she knew she was pretty and that was everything.

This demonstrates the strengths of this point of view. Oates does a masterful job of moving the camera in and around Connie, giving the reader an exterior view of Connie, at the same time conveying a sense of how Connie might actually speak, her voice (for instance, "her mother who hadn't much reason any longer to look at her own face"). What makes this different from an omniscient narrator, however, is that the thoughts and perspectives are all Connie's; we do not see this world through another, "larger," narrator's eyes. The story is told by the chatter, the highly self-conscious chatter, that dominates Connie's perception of herself and her world. Towards the end of the story, as the events of the story force her into a much deeper, even tragic awareness, the point of view also moves extremely close. But Oates is not creating a larger consciousness that is telling us about Connie; this is Connie's view of herself and—Oates's brilliant use of point of view to underscore theme—of her own consciousness as it is raised in the course of the story.

Another distant narrator is Evan S. Connell's eponymous Mrs. Bridge. In this example, too, although for very different reasons than Connie's, the author manages to convey the distance Mrs. Bridge feels from herself. And again the choice of narrator underscores the novel's thematic concerns.

> That evening, while preparing for bed, Mrs. Bridge suddenly paused with the fingertips of one hand just touching her cheek. She was seated before her dressing table in her robe and slippers and had begun spreading cold cream on her face. The touch of the cream, the unexpectedness of it—for she had been thinking deeply about how to occupy tomorrow—the swift cool touch demoralized her so completely she almost screamed.

Mrs. Bridge is thinking about "how to occupy tomorrow," one of the saddest and most revealing sentences in twentieth-century fiction. She is hardly aware of her actions, so practiced and habitual is the act of removing one mask (her make-up) with another (cold-cream)—and in the process discovering quite another mask altogether: an effective use of activity to underscore the metaphorical implications of the scene. Throughout the novel, Connell consistently refers to her as Mrs. Bridge—a method of showing just how thorough is this character's distance from herself.

Distant third allows the camera to draw in close, while also providing the capability to move some distance away. Thus the author can reveal aspects of character and character description, which a closer third or first is not pliable enough to do. This ability to move in and out, near and far, is one of its great advantages. The detachment allows for flexibility and variety.

Sometimes distant third stays really distant; the reader has no access to the characters' thoughts, emotions, or sensory impressions but has to rely on the author's use of action, gesture, and dialogue to discover what might be going on—in this it is most like an actual camera. Many of Hemingway's stories are examples of this; "Hills Like White Elephants" takes it to an effective extreme:

> "What should we drink?" the girl asked. She had taken off her hat and put it on the table.
>
> "It's pretty hot," the man said.
>
> "Let's drink beer."
>
> "*Dos cervezas*," the man said into the curtain.
>
> "Big ones?" a woman asked from the doorway.
>
> "Yes. Two big ones."
>
> The woman brought two glasses of beer and two felt pads. She put the felt pads and the beer glasses on the table and looked at the man and the girl. The girl was looking off at the line of hills. They were white in the sun and the country was brown and dry.
>
> "They look like white elephants," she said.
>
> "I've never seen one," the man drank his beer.

"No, you wouldn't have."

It can be argued that in "Hills" Hemingway employs an omniscient narrator. But to my mind, "the man" is the narrator. Hemingway's choice of this distant point of view underscores the man's distance from himself: the clueless-ness or cruelty behind what, in the story, he asks "the girl" to do, and his reaction to her distress in being asked. That is, the point of view stays resolutely outside these charac-ters, just as "the man" is resolutely distant from himself. Even the lack of names—calling the characters simply "the girl," "the man," "the woman"—enforces a distance on the reader, and here again the point of view resonates the story's thematic concerns.

The perspective shows us where they are—a train station; it shows us the surrounding scenery—the odd-shaped hills. When the woman brings the beer we see what she might see—or it could be what the man sees the woman seeing: "The girl was looking off at the line of hills." Towards the end of the story the man takes their bags to the other side of the station, and the point of view leaves the girl sitting at the table to follow him. He then has a drink by himself at the bar and watches the people "all waiting so <u>reasonably</u> for the train." Which is to say that the "girl," with whom he's just had a most unsatisfactory—from his perspective—conversation, is not being reasonable at all. But except for this one telling adverb, Hemingway keeps us distant from any inner thought. We must discern from action and dialogue what is really going on.

Used effectively, this subjectivity can engage the reader: a mystery must be ferreted out. When less success-ful, the writing can feel flat and uninspired—as if the au-thor is distant from the material. Oates and Connell and Hemingway are purposefully creating characters that are distant; as authors they are thoroughly engaged.

OMNISCIENT NARRATORS

Fred's Diner, at the junction of Interstate 70 and 37, the cutoff for St. George, Utah, had squatted belligerently, if shabbily, at that particular crossroads for four decades. Neither 76 Corporation nor Denny's had been able to bid high enough to get Fred Slade to sell, and loyal truckers stopped there still, not because the coffee was any good—it wasn't—but because it had been there for so long and they respected these things. At least the older ones did, and they passed this sense of stylistic imperative on to the younger drivers via their CB radios. "Pie at Fred's," was something they'd all agree on, and they'd stop for a piece of cherry or apple or banana cream.

It was cherry that Sam had on his mind as he bounced high above the road in his Mack, his bladder ready to burst. Fred's was only...

An omniscient point of view may utilize the techniques of sliding and of distance, but it also gives the reader the sense of a

> Omni – ALL
> +
> Scientia – KNOWLEDGE
> KNOWING ALL

larger intelligence viewing and relating the action. To be truly omniscient, such a narrator provides an overview, a perspective, an attitude.

Fred's was only three miles ahead, and Sam looked forward to Rosie serving him eggs and coffee before that pie and if he was lucky she'd join him for a snuggle in his cab, amidst all the other diesel-blowing semis. Then he'd push it all the way to L.A.

He drew up behind a battered yellow Toyota and pulled out to pass, noting the ponytail which hung halfway down the back of the man driving. The feet of a girl in the passenger seat were pressed up against the dashboard, and her legs were long and bare. Was she wearing anything at all? Shorts, maybe. Sam slowed and craned his neck for a better view. The man's mouth was twisted, he was yelling, but Sam couldn't see the girl's reaction. Nice pair of gams, though.

Sam tooted as he pulled ahead of the Toyota, *toot toooot*, like the whistle he'd blow through his lips if she could hear him, then pulled back in ahead of them and flashed his lights. The back draft from the semi as it passed almost blew the car off the road.

Jim, driving, wrenched at the wheel, and stuck his hand out the window, jerking his middle finger at the rear of the truck. The lights flashed a second time. "Jerk." He glanced over at Margie. "Maybe it's your legs he's honking at."

The component parts of the word "Omniscient" come from the Latin for All (*omni*) and Knowing (*sciencia*; from the same derivation comes our word <u>science</u>). All Knowing: that's what this perspective is. It knows things Sam can't know. It knows Sam. It can move with the back draft of his truck into Jim's car and tell us what Jim thinks, what Margie thinks, and even what they will all eventually discover.

Margie put her knuckle in her mouth and bit down hard. She would not speak, no matter what he said, she would not rise to the bait. Tears seeped down her cheeks. Her dirty hair was pulled back into a pony tail that flattened her skull and emphasized the bones of her face. Her skin was an almost translucent white. For a moment, Jim felt concern. She needed to eat. Food was the answer to her problems—their problems. He put his turn signal on, and the Toyota spun across two lanes of traffic, causing a VW to brake and a Lexus to sound its horn as the battered yellow shape sped down the off ramp and turned into a parking lot beneath the sign announcing Fred's Diner.

Margie took the knuckle out of her mouth. "What are we doing?"

"Breakfast. There ain't nothing a little food can't fix."

"Is that so," she said, but softly, so he would not hear her.

This was not the first time, nor would it be the last, that Margie would be unlucky in love, and this breakfast, at this innocuous intersection of two roads in Southern Utah, would send her life in a direction no one, not all her previous lovers, not her mother, at the moment boiling an egg in Florida, not her father, currently thrashing about in bed with his new wife, and certainly not Jim, could have predicted.

If a writer plans to use such a narrator, ideally its omniscience is established early on. In Michael Cunningham's *The Hours*, for instance, the narrator takes us to the river with Virginia Woolf, giving us a picture of her from the outside as well as her thoughts and feelings as she puts stones in the pockets of her sweater, as she walks into the river, as the river takes her; the narrator stays with her body as it moves downstream and eventually fetches up against a piling. As readers we might think we are in Woolf's point of view, but because that intelligence literally dies, we understand that here is a narrator who clearly knows more than Woolf. Omniscience—and authority—are established.

Michael Cunningham has spoken of his purpose in employing such a point of view: emulating what Woolf does in her own novels in (her phrase), "passing the baton of consciousness."

The idea of passing the baton of point of view, as in a relay, is a lovely one. Also useful in establishing omniscience is the analogy to a camera.

An "establishing shot" is a useful way to let your reader know what's in store. If you do choose to start with a "tight shot"—a moment of intense, close-up action—subsequent scenes establish the "bigger picture" you intend your narration to convey. Any "zoom" in or out or any switch in point of view should be made keeping in mind the issues of distance and proximity discussed above, so that the reader is not confused; for example, passing the point of view along with a glass of wine, or having the point of view stay in the room even though the current point of view character exits. (See "Moving the Point of View.") But just like a scene in a movie, a skillful writer can jump from the "view" through one person's eyes to the "view" through another's.

Many omniscient narrators establish their authority—their "credentials"—by giving the reader a sense of distance: a historical perspective, a philosophical insight, a geographical description. The sweep of this camera is wide and knowledgeable; the narrator (sometimes, but not necessarily, the author) lets the reader know that it knows more than any single character in the novel knows, and, in addition, can look through the eyes of anyone it chooses.

Physical or **geographical** distance is one tool with which to immediately establish a sense of omniscience; in addition, the "camera" can move in slowly to occupy a specific point of view, as Oakley Hall does in his novel, *Warlock*:

> Warlock lay on a flat, white alkali step, half encircled by the Bucksaw Mountains to the east, beneath a metallic sky. With the afternoon sun slanting down on it from over the distant peaks of the Dinosaurs, the adobe and weathered plank-and-batten, false-fronted buildings were smoothly glazed with yellow light, and sharp-cut black shadows lay like pits in the angles out of the sun.
>
> The heat of the sun was like a blanket; it had dimension and weight. The town was dust- and heat-hazed, blurred out of focus. A water wagon with a round, rust-red tank moved slowly along Main Street, spraying water in a narrow, shining strip behind it. But Warlock's dust was laid only briefly. Soon again it was churned as light as air by iron-clad wheels, by hoofs and bootheels.

Hall follows this dust and all the places it lands, allowing the reader to see Warlock, as well as the territory, mines, and roads that lead into the town "like twisted spokes to a dusty hub." Then we slowly close in on a character that will be one of the narrators (close third) in the novel:

> Dust rose, too, where there were travelers along the roads: a prospector with his burro; a group of riders coming in from San Pablo; great, high-wheeled, heavy-laden ore wagons descending from the mines... and, close in on the Welltown road, a single horseman slowly making his way up through the huge, strewn boulders towards Warlock's rim.

Thus we arrive at the perspective of John Gannon. After a space break, Hall writes,

> John Gannon rode bent tiredly forward against the slope, his hand on the dusty, sweated shoulder of the gray he had bought in Welltown, urging her up this last hill out of the malpais and over the rim, where she increased her gait at the sight of town. He glanced down the rutted trail to his right that led out to the cemetery called Boot Hill...

The verb "glancing" begins to pull us into Gannon's head. He is returning to town—his familiarity with the destination of that "rutted trail" demonstrates this—and for the duration of this chapter Hall pulls that proximity ever closer to Gannon, giving the reader details only Gannon sees, and, eventually, thoughts he thinks. And, as each subsequent chapter begins, Hall puts us into another perspective.

Here's the opening to Stephen Crane's "The Bride Comes to Yellow Sky":

> The great Pullman was whirling onward with such dignity of motion that a glance from the window seemed simply to

> prove that the plains of Texas were pouring eastward. Vast flats of green grass, dull hued spaces of mesquite and cactus, little groups of frame houses, woods of light and tender trees, all were sweeping into the east, sweeping over the horizon, a precipice.
>
> A newly married pair had boarded this coach at San Antonio. The man's face was reddened from many days in the wind and sun, and a direct result of his new black clothes was that his brick- colored hands were constantly performing in a most conscious fashion. From time to time he looked down respectfully at his attire....

An omniscient narrator allows the writer to "play God." As readers, we are given a panoramic perspective, and, at the same time, are allowed into the minds of a number of characters. In this opening paragraph of Crane's story about the demise of the Old West, the camera is a wide-angle one, a lens above the action, "zooming in" from a distance, looking at and into whatever and whomever it pleases. It also uses, in the story's first image, the theme of the story: not so much that the East is coming to the West (in the form of a bride, and all that marriage brings to a lawless society), but that the West is "pouring" towards the East.

The voice of an omniscient narrator is usually not that of a particular character, but a larger consciousness, or, at times, of the author-as-narrator, as in this excerpt from Henry James's *The Portrait of a Lady*.

> Under certain circumstances there are few hours in life more agreeable than the hour dedicated to the ceremony known as afternoon tea. There are circumstances in

which, whether you partake of the tea or
not—some people of course never do,—the
situation is in itself delightful. Those that I
have in mind in beginning to unfold this
simple history offered an admirable setting to
an innocent pastime. The implements of the
little feast had been disposed upon the lawn
of an old English country-house, in what I
should call the perfect middle of a splendid
summer afternoon... The persons concerned
in it were taking their pleasure quietly, and
they were not of the sex which is supposed to
furnish the regular votaries of the ceremony
I have mentioned. The shadows on the perfect lawn were straight and angular; they
were the shadows of an old man sitting in a
deep wicker-chair near the low table on
which the tea had been served, and of two
younger men strolling to and fro, in desul-
tory talk, in front of him. The old man had
his cup in his hand; it was an unusually
large cup, of a different pattern from the rest
of the set and painted in brilliant colours....

That simple clause, "some people of course never
do," gives the reader a sense of a narrator who will be in-
serting his opinion about other matters as well; this is one
of the things that an omniscient narrator can do.

This is a classic example of an outside narrator—
James's "I"—who intends to stand outside the action and
relate it to the reader. The reader understands immediately
that this narrator can and will go anywhere he pleases: here
the narrator ruminates on the ritual of afternoon tea, describes the forms that shadows are taking, closes in to the
unusual cup the man in the wheelchair is holding. We will

be given a perspective on, and the perspectives of, the various members of this group before Isabel Archer, the "lady" of the novel's title, appears on the scene. However, unlike the usual understanding of a first-person narrator, the story will not be "about" him, or act upon him to change him in any way.

Establishing an **historical** perspective also provides a sense of distance from the events of the story, The narrator may deliver information about the era in which the story takes place, as Jane Austen's does as she begins *Sense and Sensibility*:

> The family of Dashwood had been long settled in Sussex. Their estate was large, and their residence was at Norland Park, in the centre of their property, where, for many generations, they had lived in so respectable a manner as to engage the general good opinion of their surrounding acquaintance. The late owner of this estate was a single man who lived to a very advanced age, and who for many years of his life had a constant companion and housekeeper in his sister. But her death, which happened ten years before his own, produced a great alteration in his home; for to supply her loss, he invited and received into his house the family of his nephew Mr. Henry Dashwood, the legal inheritor of the Norland estate....

The omniscient narrator of Toni Morrison's *Beloved* establishes a very different kind of history:

> 124 was spiteful. Full of a baby's venom. The women in the house knew it and so did the children. For years each put up

with the spite in his own way, but by 1873, Sethe and her daughter Denver were its only victims. The grandmother, Baby Suggs, was dead, and the sons, Howard and Buglar, had run away by the time they were thirteen years old—as soon as merely looking in a mirror shattered it (that was the signal for Buglar); as soon as two tiny hand prints appeared in the cake (that was it for Howard). Neither boy waited to see more; another kettleful of chickpeas smoking in a heap on the floor; soda crackers crumbled and strewn in a line next to the doorsill.... No. Each one fled at once... leaving their grandmother, Baby Suggs; Sethe, their mother; and their little sister, Denver, all by themselves in the gray and white house on Bluestone Road. It didn't have a number then, because Cincinnati didn't stretch that far. In fact, Ohio had been calling itself a state only seventy years when first one brother and then the next stuffed quilt packing into his hat, snatched up his shoes, and crept away from the lively spite the house felt for them.

At this point the author pulls us into a specific point of view, as she will, sliding into and out of the minds of various characters, throughout the novel:

Baby Suggs didn't even raise her head. From her sickbed she heard them go but that wasn't the reason she lay still. It was a wonder to her that her grandsons has taken so long to realize....

Philosophical distance allows an author to create an omniscient narrator with more of a "voice," one that may offer insightful, witty, and occasionally sardonic commentary about the human natures it will depict. Here again is Jane Austen, in her famous introduction to *Pride and Prejudice*:

> It is a truth universally acknowledged that a single man in possession of a good fortune must be in want of a wife.

Such a perspective can arrive laced with irony, and as a result, a reader can feel that the writer is judging her characters, and not finding them admirable, much less likable. This attitude, while one of the dangers of omniscience, can also be part of its charm, as in J.D. Salinger's opening to "A Perfect Day for Bananafish":

> There were ninety-seven New York advertising men in the hotel, and, the way they were monopolizing the long-distance lines, the girl in 507 had to wait from noon till almost two-thirty to get her call through. She used the time, though. She read an article in a women's pocket-size magazine, called, "Sex Is Fun—or Hell." She washed her comb and brush. She took the spot out of the skirt of her beige suit. She moved the button on her Saks blouse. She tweezed out two freshly surfaced hairs in her mole. When the operator finally rang her room, she was sitting on the window seat and had almost finished putting lacquer on the nails of her left hand.
>
> She was a girl who for a ringing phone dropped exactly nothing. She looked as if her

phone had been ringing continually ever since she had reached puberty.

An omniscient narrator can also provide **psychological** distance. This does not necessarily mean that a character's history, emotions, and personality are reported in a remote and condescending manner. This narrator knows full well what any particular character is going through and can choose at any time to reveal a choice morsel of inner monologue or thought process. For instance, here's Thackeray in *Vanity Fair* on his heroine, Becky Sharp:

> For it may be remarked in the course of this little conversation (which took place as the coach rolled along lazily by the riverside) that though Miss Rebecca Sharp has twice had occasion to thank heaven, it had been, in the first place, for ridding her of some person whom she hated, and secondly, for enabling her to bring her enemies to some sort of perplexity or confusion; neither of which are very amiable motives for religious gratitude...

John Fowles, in *The French Lieutenant's Woman*, both utilizes and parodies the "god-narrator" of eighteenth- and nineteenth-century novelists. He often reminds the reader that he is creating these characters and their story, At the end of Chapter Twelve he writes, "Who is Sarah? Out of what shadows does she come?" and offers this answer as Chapter Thirteen begins:

> I do not know. This story I am telling is all imagination. These characters I create never existed outside my own mind. If I have pretended until now to know my characters'

minds and innermost thoughts, it is because
I am writing in (just as I have assumed some
of the vocabulary and "voice" of) a conven-
tion universally accepted at the time of my
story: that the novelist stands next to God.

...Certainly I intended at this stage
(*Chap. Thirteen—unfolding of Sarah's true
state of mind*) to tell all—or all that matters... (but) I know in the context of my
book's reality that Sarah would never have
brushed away her tears and leaned down and
delivered a chapter of revelation. She would
instantly have turned, had she seen me there
just as the old moon rose, and disappeared
into the interior shadows...

This creation of character, this manipulating of
events, is what all authors do, but usually we struggle to
keep the artifice from our readers. Fowles, in the text and
even with footnotes, gleefully takes time away from the
story to explain his characters' nineteenth-century psy-
chologies to us. When Charles, amateur archeologist, takes
a post-prandial grog with Doctor Grogan, amateur scientist
(and both enthralled by the newly-published theories of
Darwin), Fowles begins to bring their evening and the
chapter to a close by writing, "new cheroots were lit; and a
lengthy celebration of Darwin followed. They ought, one
may think, to have been humbled by the great truths they
were discussing; but I am afraid the mood in both of
them—and in Charles especially, when he finally walked
home in the small hours of the morning—was one of ex-
alted superiority, intellectual distance above the rest of
their fellow creatures."

This "I" narrator is not changed in or by the course
of the story, but is creating and manipulating events. In *The*

French Lieutenant's Woman, Fowles even goes so far as to give us two endings—one "happy" ("Victorian") and less "true," and therefore less satisfying, than the other, but leaves it up to the reader to decide which she prefers.

Part of the genius of the novel is that in spite of (and because of) the author/narrator's interruptions and ruminations, it reads in a most compelling way: we feel that these lives <u>are</u> "real," and that they are unfolding <u>in spite of</u> the author's manipulations. This is because when Fowles does move into his characters' minds, occupying them or moving among them in close third, he utilizes authentic dialogue and precise and true action and gesture; he is sympathetic to their plight—even as he is clearly creating that plight. We understand that he has a hand in everything; nevertheless, the story and the characters live on in the reader's mind.

The popularity of the narrator-as-god, and that god-like creature being white and male, waned in the early part of the twentieth century. Such narrators began to seem paternal, if not patronizing. Also, perhaps with the rise of psychology in the twentieth century, readers became interested in figuring out for themselves what makes a character tick, rather than having everything explained to them by a god-like narrator. With the advent of cinema, and its contributions to what is considered effective and engaging storytelling, readers want their stories vivid, to be shown to them rather than told—as omniscient narrators often tend to do. Readers want to figure out character and motivation for themselves, rather than being dictated to or having events explained.

Whatever the reasons, except for thrillers and historical fiction and the like, the omniscient narrator fell somewhat out of favor. But the pendulum is swinging, and it seems to be coming back into vogue again, in part perhaps because of what I jokingly refer to as my Colonial Theory of Point of View. In any case, it behooves the serious writer to have a sense of its component parts. Anything is possible when its elements are understood, and putting those elements to use is done with purpose. Here are a few examples of authors and books that do that.

INTRIGUING USES OF NARRATOR

Louis B. Jones accomplishes a remarkable feat in his novel *California's Over*. His first-person narrator, Baelthon, has the emotional and temporal distance from the story to become an omniscient narrator. Baelthon knows the characters in his life so intimately that he can move to their perspectives. So although the story is ostensibly a first-person tale, Baelthon is often a character looked at through the point of view of other characters. How Jones effects these shifts in perspective employs sliding the perspective in unique ways.

An example: Baelthon, looking for work, meets Wendy and her mother. This passage begins with Baelthon's first-person point of view, in which much of the story so far has been told. Observe how Jones slides the point of view from Baelthon's first person, to Wendy's third, something that would seem to be almost impossible to do.

> When Wendy first met me **(Baelthon, first person)**, she found me dislikable simply as a block against the light. I was the first of many intruders she was expecting, in an already humiliated time. Not only was she under the peculiar humiliation of having to leave the only home she'd ever known, but, too, at that moment, she believed the box in her hands contained her father's cremated ashes. **(The verb "believed" begins to move the POV; still, this could be information Baelthon is privy to, knowing Wendy—as we discover,**

through the novel. he does.) They had been stashed here and simply forgotten, under a folded old tie-dyed silk parachute on the billiard table. McGUFFIN was printed on all four sides of the box—it was the name of a funeral home over the hill in the suburbs. On a top flap of the box, in Magic Marker script, the name *J. Farmican* was written—the name of the occupant. **(All this information could be Baelthon's knowledge of Wendy—or have we moved to her POV?)**

"Is this..." she couldn't say it (*Is this... Dad?*), prevented by the unfair comedy of it. But she could see she'd guessed right, by her mother's characteristic humorous, stabbed drop of the shoulders, as she moved into the depth of the storeroom. "Wendy, isn't today a school day?" **(By now we're pretty definitely in Wendy's POV, especially the observation of her mother's gesture; and yet, these are still details that Baelthon could know.)**

Involuntarily she drew the— remarkably light!—box closer in her arms. "I thought these were"—she lowered her voice—"scattered." **(The "remarkably light" box anchors us completely; she is the one hefting it.)**

This section moves on as the mother continues to speak to Wendy, and the reader is aware, to some degree, that since Baelthon is reporting it, of course he is there, watching the exchange. But then Wendy leaves, taking the point of view with her:

... she left, heading for daylight, striding up the incline with a gait that, she could never forget, was so graceless she seemed totally unrelated to her mother. She hadn't once raised her eyes to look at the employee **(the "employee" is Baelthon—the transfer is now complete)**, out of a numbness that must be fatigue... In the long basement tunnel, the stone floor's upward incline, Egyptian-feeling, made her bow her head, against the strap of a headache. **(The headache pulls us all the way inside Wendy—and we go now where she goes, leaving Baelthon and his point of view, for the time being, behind.)**

Karen Joy Fowler, in *The Jane Austen Book Club*, creates a sly and witty perspective, the book club itself. The "we" of her first person plural narrator is able to both give us a large perspective of the characters as well as the club, while allowing her to rotate in close third, and even at times in first, among the individual club members. A brief example (Grigg is the man in the otherwise all-female book club):

> The phone rang and Grigg went to get it. "Bianca," we heard. There was genuine pleasure in his voice, but not that kind of pleasure. Just a friend, we thought. "Can I call you back? My Jane Austen book club is here."
>
> But we told him to take the call. We were done with our discussion and could let ourselves out. We carried our plates and our glasses to the kitchen, said good-bye to the cat, and tiptoed away. Grigg was talking about his mother as we left; apparently she had a birthday coming up. Not a friend, then, we thought, but a sister.

> After we'd gone, Grigg talked to Bianca about us. "I *think* they like me..."

In the aforementioned *Warlock*, a novel that dramatizes why society will eventually insist on order, and then need law to keep that order, Oakley Hall, in a tour-de-force of point of view, rotates a first, several close thirds, distant, and at times omniscient narrators, echoing one of the novel's themes: acts of individuals have broader, societal effects.

In *The Blind Assassin*, Margaret Atwood employs several narrators, including a novel within the novel, in a tightrope walk of point of view, with an unexpected and most satisfying resolution and explanation for their use.

One of the narrators of Jennifer Egan's aforementioned novel, *Look at Me*, is a model whose beautiful face has been destroyed in an accident and then re-constructed. Egan rotates her first-person narration with sliding and several close thirds, underscoring this character's obsession, and by extension the obsession of the culture in which she lives, with being looked at but not, perhaps, being seen.

Another novel whose resolution—in this case its last line—both satisfyingly underscores and explains the choice of narration, is *Snow Falling on Cedars*. As David Guterson begins his novel, the point of view seems to be the town's; it is both everywhere and not particularly anywhere. As the story unfolds, it moves intimately into any number of perspectives, and is definitely omniscient. But with the novel's last line, when we are in the point of view of the newspaper owner/reporter, Ishmael, we get a glimmer of the possibility that there is in fact one person that might have been able to know all the details, capable of being intimate, and nosy, and imaginative. This, perhaps, is the "authority" that has told us the tale.

IN CONCLUSION

Many novelists have written books from one point of view only to start over and change the narration from first to third person, or move the point of view from Margie's to Jim's. Sometimes they return to their original impulse, having learned a great deal of necessary information about their characters and their story by the work they did. Or perhaps they decide to rotate the points of view. Or they start with omniscience to set the scene, and then slide or rotate amongst two or three narrators.

Sit by your bookshelf and pull out a pile of novels. Leaf through them. Determine if a book in narrated by the same character all the way through its pages. If not, when does the perspective change? Does it rotate? Slide? Is the authority telling the tale an omniscient? What tone does that omniscience take?

Begin to read with a new eye. Watch what writers do with point of view, and how they create it. Keep an eye on the use of language and syntax. Be aware of grammar. Vocabulary. Perhaps even the punctuation is underscoring some element of the point of view. Be aware of voice. If you get caught up in the plot (a good sign) remind yourself to periodically check and see if the story is still being told by the same narrator. If not, when did it change? How did the author accomplish it so that you didn't notice?

Examine the points of view you've chosen for your own narratives. Is it always a similar person? Might it be interesting to experiment with someone different, to put on a mask or persona? Have you chosen the most effective perspective? If you're bogged down, you might ask if there is someone else in your cast of characters who might be more engaging, or who might have an odd and useful perspective on the action. If you're working in first person, try a bit of the story in third, and vice versa. Try the perspective of someone else in that particular chapter. These experiments are particularly useful if you're having trouble with character, plot, or the overall movement of your story.

Who tells your story is vital. Point of view is the pedal tone of a story—the low, profound note that sustains through the pages. It also provides reason for the selection of all the other notes that go into creating a work of fiction: the specific detail, the appropriate language, the figure of speech, vocabulary, punctuation. Who is it that is doing the viewing, how does he think, how does he speak, how does he see, hear, feel—above all, how does he (and these are, of course, selections the author makes) convey these things to the reader? It is worth the thought and effort, the trial and error, it takes to discover who that character is, and the necessary devotion to craft to develop and sustain that voice.

PUT IT TO WORK

EXERCISES:

18. Some Rainy Day (page 253)

17. Through Eyes That Slide (page 252)

10. Through Other Eyes (Getting Some Perspective) (page 235)

19. Through Distant Eyes (page 255)

20. Through Omniscient Eyes (page 257)

16. Through Opposite Eyes (Other Side of the Picture) (page 250)

12. Setting up a Scene (page 239)

It might also be useful to look at:

3.   Objectives & Obstacles (page 221) and / or

6.   Checklist for a Scene (page 227) and / or

25. What Does This Scene Need to Accomplish? (page 265)

THE COLONIAL THEORY OF POINT OF VIEW

Once upon a time…

It has often occurred to me that British writers, both canonical and contemporary, seem to have an especial ability with the omniscient perspective: Fielding, Dickens, and Austen; Forster, Woolf, and Waugh; Byatt and Barker. In contrast, American writers (I classify the expatriate Henry James as more English than American) seem to have early on developed an affinity for the narrower perspectives of first person or close third, although these narrators may emerge onto the page in highly diverse ways: Melville's "Call me Ishmael"; Twain's "You don't know about me without you have read…"; Faulkner's "Through the fence, between the curling flower spaces, I could see them hitting."

Perhaps England's writers were responding to the notion that "Britannia Rules the Waves"; after all, during the six-, seven-, eight-, and nineteenth centuries, Britain colonized the world. I see it seeing itself as this small but shining emerald at the top of the globe, looking out and down at the rest of the world, which looked up to its shining example (according to it) for everything culturally vital. After so many centuries of being top (white) dog, perhaps this tendency to view from a larger perspective became almost atavistic, bred in the bone as it were, and made its way, as often as not humorously, into the perspectives of their novels, as when Dickens avows, "It was the best of times, it was the worst of times..." and Austen proposes that "It is a truth universally acknowledged that a single man in possession of a good fortune must be in search of a wife..." and Galsworthy maintains that "Those privileged to be present at a family festival of the Forsytes have seen that charming and instructive sight—an upper middle class family in full plumage..."

Early settlers of America were usually looking for some form of *dis*connection—moving away from a mother country, or out to unsettled land, seeking opportunities to make a new life, an individual mark, far from the collective empires they'd left. While Wharton and other American authors may have employed the vast perspectives of their peers across the Atlantic pond, perhaps this attitude of "don't tread on me" influenced the points of view put to use by some American writers, such as those quoted above: Twain's Huckleberry, Melville's Ishmael, and Faulkner's Curly.

I also noticed that Latin American writers—certainly their celebrated and well-known authors, but also students in classes with little or no writing experience—moved easily amidst and looked through the points of view of not only other characters, but those of ghosts, birds, butterflies, candles, fire. Who doesn't remember with joy Marquez's *One Hundred Years of Solitude* and Allende's *House of Spirits*. It seemed to me that their writing mirrored their cultural understandings, as Britain's did theirs, and America's theirs.

This limited and highly-subjective discussion does not include the many other cultures whose people came to America, except to say that at first, for the most part, they strove for assimilation: *Let my voice be yours*; and in that effort perhaps their writers did not immediately strive for a larger perspective, nor a unique one. In this America became not so much a melting pot but a sort of stir-fry: a coming together while maintaining discrete forms and taste. Only gradually, in the twentieth century, did this begin to announce itself in voices, female and other-cultural, relating their views of the American experience. Tan, Morrison, Ehrlich, Lahiri and so many others.

And all of this also has to do with shifts in philosophy, of course: swerves and upheavals in religion and science and psychology and politics. Now America has become its own colonizing force in the world. Has this contributed to the emphasis and exploration we see of the omniscient point of view by our own native writers? Americans have now become the "top" of the world. (And although we seem to have an appreciation for, or at least grant respect to, the perspectives of others, is it only "pretty to think so"?) In any case, in my reading in the last decade, I have noticed many more writers playing with omniscient perspectives. This may merely mirror my own interests and abilities to perceive point of view. And there are no doubt myriad explanations besides this limited and mostly-amusing notion. But there you have it: the Colonial Theory of Point of View.

MOVING THE POINT OF VIEW

As a writer becomes interested in working with and manipulating point of view, questions arise about when and why and how to transfer it from one character to another. When and why are important things to consider, as sliding the point of view around can come across as simply lazy: the writer just moves from one "head" to another, to tell us each character's thoughts, rather then doing the hard work of staying in one character's perceptions and revealing to the reader, through action, gesture, and dialogue, what might be going on with the other characters in the scene, and thereby engaging the reader in discovering these things. And sometimes, all that leaping about from point of view to point of view obfuscates other necessary elements of a scene: the objectives of a character, for instance, can get fuzzy if the writer moves too often in and out of her head. In addition, the writer-objective can be diffused through too much moving about. But whether one is interested in a sliding point of view or its larger cousin, omniscience, moving the point of view is a way to convey the perspectives of several characters in a single scene, and, as many literary examples demonstrate, can be a delightful way to get a story told. To that end, here are a few ideas about how to effect the transition of the point of view without jarring the reader.

AN OBJECT GETS TRANSFERRED AND SO DOES THE POV:

Stacy opened the envelope and scanned the single sheet it contained with what she hoped would look like casual interest, even as her heart began to thud. There it was, her own damning signature. With a dismissive shrug, she handed the page to Frank, who snatched and read it greedily, thrilled at the words so irrevocably typed onto the thick, water-marked bond. "Well, well," he said, folding it up, delighting in the panic that flared in her eyes. "What about that, Stacy? What about that?"

MOVEMENT CAN ALSO BE USED TO HELP THE SHIFT, AS CAN A SENSORY PERCEPTION:

Emma's skirts rustled as she moved towards Mobius, who stood in the doorway, arms folded. She kept her eyes low, not wanting to acknowledge those narrowed eyes and that lifted lip. But he wasn't going to let her past; she had to turn sideways to slip by. The gardenia-like perfume she wore rose from her skin as her skirt lapped over the top of his boots, and he almost groaned. Delicious, impossible creature. He turned and caught her elbow as she tried to slip from the room.

A GLANCE, OR AN EXCHANGE OF LOOKS, CAN MOVE THE POV:

> Those freckles, tossed like confetti across her cheeks, should mar Marianne's beauty, not add to it, but Lasky wanted to kiss the one that perched just to the left of her nose. He smiled, and she turned away, hatred flowing from her like the green monster she knew it to be.

Anything "interior" to a character helps to slide the point of view. Aroma, thought, sensation, and the like can be used to firmly and immediately ground us in another perspective.

THE POV CAN BE TRANSFERRED TO A CHARACTER WHO STAYS IN A ROOM AS THE ORIGINAL POV CHARACTER EXITS:

> At intermission, Corinne ran into the Caldwells at the bar in the lower lobby and demanded their opinion. "I'm not sure yet," Bonnie said, tossing back that well-coiffed mane of hers. "I'm waiting, don't you know, for the end of the play before I pass judgment?" Mitch nodded. As always, he would be unable to make up his mind until Bonnie had her opinions in place and her review written. "Well, I think it's an insipid piece of crap," Corinne said, and delighted in the shocked glances she got from those animatedly yakking and imbibing around them. She almost guffawed as Mitch and Bonnie simultaneously sipped their wine; the move looked choreographed: glasses moving up, pause for gulps, glasses moving down. "Well, see you afterwards at the paaahty," she said, waving gaily. "Ta ta."

Bonnie took another swallow of the too-sweet white and watched Corinne's trim black rear-end swivel up the carpeted steps and out of sight. "Jesus," she said. "Who on earth does she think she is?" Mitch murmured one of his irritating non-specific pieces of insipid commentary. Bonnie swallowed the last of the wine. "Makes me want to give the stupid play a rave, just to spite her. And for God's sake, Mitch, form your own opinion this time, would you?"

A SENSORY PERCEPTION CAN MOVE THE POV.

The late afternoon sun fell upon Claude, harrowing his fields, and he paused to pull from around his neck the stiff and dry kerchief he'd dampened, just an hour ago, in the nearby crick. He used it to scrub his forehead, which was wet with sweat and dark with dust, and then looked at the kerchief and thought about the dust that he'd come from and the dust to which he was destined to return, with nothing in between but all this work. "Get on, Harvey," he said and Harvey flicked his tail and lifted his huge hooves and got on, heading straight into the sun which was sinking, ever more large and red as it descended, and against its angry orb the house at the far end of the field stood out, a squat dark shape, with a plug that was the chimney, and a line heading out from one side that was the clothesline. Worthy was there, getting the laundry off before night came with all its dew, bringing in the sheets that she and Claude would lie on that night.

She slipped the final clothespin off the sheet's hem and tucked the edge under her chin to begin the process of folding, wondering why Claude was so restless these nights, why it was that she sometimes heard him breathing harshly in a way that if it was a sound from any other man than Claude she would think had to do with crying.

Or

In the old Craftsman-style bungalow a block off the beach in Santa Monica, Sally Reynolds typed rapidly, the keyboard making satisfying, deep-noted taps as the sentences rolled out of her mind and onto the screen; she was deep into the conclusion, and in just a few moments would be able to press SEND and the story would zip through the lines that connected her computer to that of her boss, Len Benatelli, in his high-rise steel-and-glass office in downtown LA. Then began the distant, familiar gut-clenching sound of a million glasses jangling together, wine glasses or maybe it was all those double-paned windows between her and the epicenter of whatever was coming at her, shaking her house and her desk and making her keyboard slide sideways, the sound moving towards her and then, as the shaking climaxed and moved off, the jangling moved too, off to Culver City, where Mitty stopped in the midst of feeding her seven Abyssinian cats, holding the can of Feline Frolic that Precious loved. What on earth they would do if the house fell down around them? Then the shaking and

the sound of a million wine glasses tapping
together, not breaking, just lightly tapping,
ting, ting, ting, moved towards West Hollywood. It swept along Melrose Avenue, where
Filco, in her little boutique, scrambled into
an arched doorway, arms out to both sides
for comfort, the hangers of her designer
dresses clanging together and all her windows about to just bust open, and then came
the shaking, which reminded her of that
movie where the guy was electrocuted and
you got to watch, and she slid down to sit on
the quaking floor and put her head to her
knees as if she could press away the idea that
life was pretty awful everywhere on the
planet at this moment, which was pretty
much the headline that Len Benatelli felt like
writing, as high in his office ten miles east on
Alvarado Avenue he edited the copy of the
ninth of the ten stories that had to get to
press *right now*, all bad news. And then the
forty-six-times-two panes of his fourteenth-
floor office (it was really the thirteenth, except they skipped that number in the eleva-
tors), began to quiver and bend and in spite
of what a ridiculous a maneuver it was, considering the number of floors above him that
could come down upon him, and the number
of floors beneath him through which he
could fall, he dove beneath his desk.

These are just a few suggestions and examples. As
you will see as you closely observe how writers put point of
view to work, some authors transfer the point of view
whenever and wherever they want to, in the middle of a

page, a paragraph, even a sentence. Ultimately it's a matter of that intangible thing called "authority."

PUT IT TO WORK

EXERCISES:

CREATING SCENE AND STORY

Stanislavski, the acting-technique theorist and teacher, called the through-line of a character's need or desire the "super-objective"; it encompasses the overall arc of the character and the plot in which she is enmeshed. In the world of theatre, the playwright has done this work, and part of the job of an actor or director is to find—or to interpret—what this is. As actor and director set to work, they seek out what has been layered into scene after scene, looking for clues about what not only drives the character but where her nature might take her and what is in the way of her accomplishing those objectives. The actor/director infers and discovers information from what the playwright has implied or stated outright in the text.

Fiction writers (as well as writers of non-fiction and memoir) must also work from the inside out, stating, showing, and implying what we want our readers to discover and interpret. A character's objective(s) is only one of many elements that must be revealed, but it is one of the most important. What a character wants illustrates her nature.

That want, and what is in the way of her grasping it, have everything to do with the plot in which she and the reader are engaged. So it is imperative that an author determine those objectives, and the earlier the better.

This is work some writers do as before they sit down to compose; they write extensive character studies and a plot outline, determining objectives and obstacles, as well as listing the specific scenes the story will need, before they launch into the actual writing. Other authors write as a way of, or on the way to, discovering these elements: they come to know aspects of their characters and objectives and even of their plot by allowing or asking the characters to reveal their objectives; even the outcome of the story might be unknown for some time to an author who works in this way. And there are many writers who balance somewhere between these two methods. However a writer approaches this necessary work, there is no story until it is accomplished.

It is not enough to tell the reader, even if we choose to deliver the information in such a way, that *Alex wants revenge* or *Alex wants to find peace.* We must make Alex's objectives clear (and Alex may want both of these things); we must layer in the revenge, or the need for peace, showing how these manifest, in scene after scene, in small ways and big, throughout the story.

Scenes that don't go anywhere can turn out to serve a vital function the drafting process: writing them can help you explore backstory or discover and refine character, or even figure out where the plot wants to go—or cannot go—next. On the other hand, it might be effective to list what you think the scene needs to accomplish before you set out to compose it.

Which is how a story is built: scene by scene.

Reading and writing are acts that happen sequentially. We don't have the option, as we do with "fade-in" or "lights up" to offer a great deal of information in a moment—and not only visually, but aurally. A fade-in might give us the sweep of the Golden Gate Bridge, a packed Volkswagen heading into the City, and on the soundtrack an Italian aria being sung slightly off-key but with gusto; as the camera pulls closer to the car we realize the driver is the singer... This might establish something like, "someone of perhaps Italian heritage, someone who knows opera, is arriving in San Francisco and is happy about it." (You had to read this sequentially, word by word—imagine seeing it; better yet, rent the movie *Serpico* and watch for yourself how much work is done in the opening minute of this movie.)

Or, in the darkness of a theatre comes the sound of African drums, multi-layered, driving and complex, and then the lights rise on a living room containing a huge couch and matching armchair covered by the skins of zebra and cougar; various horned animal heads leer from the walls, there is a fur carpet with the bear's head still attached... the door bell rings and waltzing across the stage is a young African woman wearing a turban and a black and white maid's uniform with a very short skirt, carrying a feather duster, which she uses to flick dust from the eye of a stuffed wildebeest.... Here again you've had to read it sequentially but many viewers would understand several things immediately: In this world, which may or not be in another country, there are money and a big-game hunter, and perhaps women in this world, like the stuffed and mounted animals, are treated as objects... All this before whoever is at the door enters and dialogue begins to reveal further information. And what the audience will discover, when this character enters, is what that character wants, and/or what that African maid does, and what stands in the way of their getting it…

Writers do all this using the miracle of black marks on a white page, and the process of discovery for a reader happens in a particular and sequential order. Readers can't take it in all at once. They have to move across (or up/down) the page, taking in the letters that create words, words that create sentences. Sentences create paragraphs and dialogue and description and gesture and action, aroma and emotion: page follows page and scene follows scene to create the story.

Perhaps you can visualize a sequence of boxes marching across a page, each one complete to itself but connected to ones on either side, and certainly connected, in some way, to many of the boxes preceding and certainly ones ahead. Some element gets launched in a scene that must finish in that scene (for it to be a scene), but that element must also carry energy and information into the next scene, and in many cases all the way to the end of the story. We refer to the arc of a scene: its beginning, middle and end. We refer to the arc of a chapter, the arc of a character, the arc of the story itself. All of these revolve around being clear about what a character wants, and what is in the way of her getting what she wants.

Note: Just because a character wants something does not mean it's healthy, or good, or that she gets it: For her to not get what she (thinks she) wants is often far more satisfying—for her and for the reader. But we have to start with a strong want.

And now to Part Two of this equation: A character must not only have an objective, there must be an <u>obstacle</u> in the way of attaining that objective. There must be cross-purposes.

Clearly, that Alex wants revenge means that something was done to make her feel she needs it; that Alex wants peace means that she is currently not peaceful. It's also clear that Alex has not been able to yet wreak revenge; something's in the way of that, just as there is an obstacle to her attaining peace. If she had accomplished revenge, or if she were peaceful, the story would be over, or would not be able to begin.

OBJECTIVE & OBSTACLE

Objective & Obstacle are what create a scene. Conflict. Tension.

Tension is created by presenting a character with a strong need or want—"high stakes"—and then placing something in the way of her getting what she wants.

Sad but true: We do our yoga, drink our chamomile tea, remind ourselves to breathe in moments of stress... but what a reader wants IS stress. They want tension.

This tension, these conflicts, force the writer to create a series of scenes to resolve or (at least temporarily) end, the tension. And these scenes, mounting one after another, create story.

What's in the way of a given objective is usually dramatized in the form of another character, and his wants. Sometimes the obstacle is weather, of course, or a disaster: the cows freeze to death in the blizzard; the tornado destroys the bank, and Uncle John's will along with it.... In these cases some aspect of a character's nature needs to be overcome or put to use, and that effort is the obstacle, which the weather or the disaster may symbolize in some way; and how he solves that dilemma becomes his objective. One person's objective is not always thwarted by another character's exactly opposite want. Often obstacles are at oblique angles to the objectives: Joe has made reservations for an anniversary dinner; his unsuspecting and forgetful wife is at the gym doing her workout. Mary wants to go to the zoo; Betty wants to go to the movies. Jerry arrives with flowers, intending to ask Sue to marry him; Sue can't even find a vase for the flowers because she's misplaced her glasses, and spends the next half-hour looking for them (because she has a good idea of Jerry's intention, and dreads it).

A character is often working out something in her nature that is manifested in the needs of another character. That is, the obstacle within one character is dramatized in the form of the objective of another character.

One way to discover this, a way to dig deep into a story and the needs of its characters, is to ask "Why?"

ASKING WHY

Asking "Why?" is something an acting teacher, Ed Hastings, advised us to do in a scene class (yes, actors work on scenes, too, breaking them down into their component parts so that they can approach an entire play with some skill). Asking "Why?" can help create a full and rounded character. Often the answers are available in the text of the script, supplied by the playwright. Sometimes the director helps supply them. Sometimes the actor invents bits and pieces as he creates his character.

A fiction writer can also ask "Why?" as a way to delve into his characters, to help figure out what drives them, and what they really want; it is that dance between objective and obstacle that helps us discover and propel plot. For instance (from a novel on which I am currently working):

> Why does Alex want revenge—and peace?
> She is angry. She is furious, at all men, past and present. Her world has become distilled into a cesspool of resentment.
> Why?

Because her daughter killed herself.

Why?

Because her daughter was molested while at summer camp. Alex didn't see the signs of depression that led to suicide until it was too late.

Why? Because she was busy. Why? Because she is ambitious. Why? Because she's trying to prove something to herself about her capabilities. Why? Because she feels her father, Buchanan, doesn't respect her.

Why? Buchanan was disappointed—she's an only child—that Alex wasn't born a boy, and through most of her very successful career Alex has suffered under the idea that only her father's good opinion, and in some way becoming the boy/man he wanted, would make her "complete." (Her marriage is another bucket of worms.) The fact that she lost her daughter as a result of this deep desire is destroying her.

Why?

Her daughter's death has forced her to realize this goal is unattainable.

Why? Because she has to face that it's ultimately not about Buchanan; she is lacking confidence in herself—as a woman, a paucity she passed on to her daughter.

An objective is always tied to a larger need in the character.

When we dig in this deep we may find something that can be probed even more deeply—something that is not answered with Why? but with What? Not only did Alex's character begin to emerge (surprising me, I might add), what drives her began to emerge also, as did ways in which she might be able to accomplish her objective. Without bringing her daughter back to life, might she be able to find peace? Will she, in fact, still want revenge?

Some of this work may turn out to be unessential—or not included—in your manuscript; some may turn out to be only tacitly present; some of it will raise issues that demand dramatization. But when we have figured out what a character wants, or a character needs (not always the same thing), and why, the plot itself begins to emerge with more clarity. This clarity informs what scenes are needed, as well as what the characters will want in and from each scene.

With a clearer sense of what a given scene needs to push forward, many writers at this point make a list of the scenes they know they will dramatize (establishing an author-objective, if you will). The list may also include information about where the scene will take place, who is in it, and what information will be established and/or pushed forward by the scene. For instance:

> Buchanan's house. Alex makes dinner which her father, as always, doesn't eat; they drink Macallan's in his living room where he as-always sits amid piles of books (he reads from one) and chocolate bars. Establish Buchanan's reputation as scholar. Also how long Alex's mother's been dead, how she kept them from fighting, how her absence is a palpable loss still. Establish big-time lecture Alex will be giving and Buchanan's dismissal of it; she does not rise to the bait, consciously (a change for her!), because she imagines, ghost-like, her mother's face; instead she says good-night, goes to her childhood bedroom, and calls her ex-husband. (The next scene).

→   Objective for Alex: Establish her credentials. Obstacle: Buchanan has his own career he talks about.

→   Objective for Buchanan: Let Alex know she's loved and respected.
Obstacle: Can't heave the words into his mouth.

Once we have our objectives, we can place our characters in settings that will make those wants clear, or heighten the stakes, or underscore aspects of personality and status. In those settings, once we start working on the dialogue that pushes forward those wants, we give our characters activity; we provide them with action and gesture in order to keep the dialogue active, to reveal how they say what they say: tone. We maintain sense of place and thereby the point of view.

Utilizing setting and activity and gesture and behavior in a given scene keeps the "camera" of point of view running and active. Too often, once a writer gives his characters dialogue, the setting and activity, however carefully selected, get dropped from the scene. The reader gets more of a tape-recorder on the scene, a transcript of conversation, which doesn't keep the point of view alive, nor let us see the characters in action.

While the dialogue must reflect the characters' wants, it should not always speak directly to or of those wants. We all talk around what we hope to get, by bringing up other things first: how pretty someone looks, what a terrific presentation they gave; we find some topic upon which we can agree before the subject is launched upon which we cannot.

Keep in mind, too, the amount of work that can be done between lines of dialogue: what isn't said; or the gesture that is used or the activity engaged in, instead of a reply. We often answer a question with another question. We often don't directly answer direct questions—and of course sometimes we do. Sometimes what seems to be a conversation is a series of sentences that reflect two individual's obsessions (objectives): neither is responding to what the other one is saying.

With all of this in mind, let's take a look at the beginning of Anne Tyler's *The Accidental Tourist.*

"THEY MIGHT HAVE BEEN RETURNING FROM TWO ENTIRELY DIFFERENT TRIPS."

As the novel begins, Macon and Sarah are driving home early from a vacation at a beach where they were supposed to spend a week, but "neither of them had the heart for it." Sarah wears a beach dress, Macon a formal summer suit; Sarah has been in the sun, Macon has largely stayed out of it; "They might have been returning from two entirely different trips." It begins to rain. Sarah expresses her concern, to which Macon replies, "I don't mind a little rain."

We understand that Tyler has placed two very different people in the "car" of this marriage. In addition, Sarah would like to slow down or stop; Macon's intention is to keep going. Tyler also establishes the growing storm in the relationship. ("Just past the start of the divided highway," she writes a few sentences later, "... the sky grew almost black... drops spattered the windshield.")

We have a setting. Two objectives and two exactly opposite obstacles. Tension—growing tension. As the chapter unfolds, this intensifies. Reflecting this, the storm through which they are driving grows worse, although Macon keeps "a steady speed." As they observe other cars waiting it out by the side of the road, Macon speeds along, "his hands relaxed on the wheel." When "great lashings of water (fling) themselves at the windshield," Macon switches the windshield wipers to high. Eventually, "a wide lake, it seemed, in the center of the highway crashed against the underside of the car and slammed it to the right," Tyler writes, but even then Macon is unfazed; he "pumped his brakes and drove on."

In the midst of the storm, as Sarah tries to find various ways to get him to stop, Macon tells her that he drives according to a "system," to which she replies, "You and your systems!" As he still won't respond to requests that they "stop and wait it out," she says: "I don't know that you really care that much."

> Macon said, "Care?"
>
> "I said to you the other day, I said, 'Macon, now that Ethan's dead I sometimes wonder if there's any point to life.' Do you remember what you answered?"
>
> "Well, not offhand," Macon said.
>
> "You said, 'Honey, to tell the truth, it never seemed to me there was all that much point to begin with.' Those were your exact words."
>
> "Um..."
>
> "And you don't even know what was wrong with that."
>
> "No, I guess I don't," Macon said.

Macon's echo of the word, "care" seems a bit hollow; we also make the huge discovery that someone named Ethan, someone clearly close to them, has died. The mention of Ethan is layered effectively into the dialogue; it's only when we later hear his name mentioned a second time that we understand he is their son.

The reader is caught up in the conflicts—what is right and what might be wrong about these characters' perspectives and actions. With the information that their son has died, we are also sympathetic to both sides of the matter. We lean in as readers, worrying about these characters even as we continue to see that each of them is resolute in what they want. Macon wants to "keep going." Sarah to "stop and wait it out." This refers to the drive they are on in this particular scene and of course it refers to the larger needs—and their character traits—that will affect and drive the novel as a whole.

Now, to make it a scene, someone needs to get what s/he wants, or to not get what s/he wants, in some decisive way. Here's how Tyler accomplishes this:

> "Also," he said, "if you don't see any point to life I can't figure why a rainstorm would make you nervous."
>
> Sarah slumped in her seat.
>
> "Will you look at that!" he said. "A mobile home's washed clear across that trailer park."
>
> "Macon, I want a divorce," Sarah told him.

And so Macon finally stops. He pulls off the road. Sarah has accomplished her objective. But Macon's objective—to keep going, "you know I drive according to a system"—is thoroughly routed. He does not have a system for what is now launched in the novel and in his life. This scene, and this incident, launches subsequent scenes, and ultimately Macon's "wake-up," dramatized by the novel.

Thus, out of the original set of cross-purposes, out of one set of conflicting wants, emerge all kinds of other conflicting wants: Plot. Story.

ARC OF A SCENE

Each scene the author selects to dramatize must <u>push some aspect of the story forward</u>. (This is how and why we select which scenes to dramatize and which to simply narrate or summarize.)

However established, cross-purposes are necessary. A scene pursues the given objective and in the course of the scene the objective is attained or it is thwarted. Either way—unless it is the last few pages of a book—the scene then sets in motion subsequent scenes; what we discover in the course of one scene launches tension that suffuses the story for pages to come.

In the scene just discussed—also a chapter—from *The Accidental Tourist*, the arc of these exactly-contrary objectives and obstacles, the deep cross-purposes of these two characters, is outlined and followed every step of the way. Although the objective that Sarah ultimately comes to, "I want a divorce," could be said to be a new objective, in fact it's a continuation of the one she's been asking for throughout the scene: she wants to STOP.

In some scenes, however, the objectives may change part way through, as some new information comes to hand for one or both of the characters. In a subsequent scene in Tyler 's novel, Macon is leaving for a trip and has to board Edward, a dog that belonged to his now-deceased son. The dog, also grieving, has taken to biting people, and as a result, the kennel Macon usually uses won't take him. Macon is literally en route to his plane; he has a pressing need: board the dog. He pulls into the Meow-Bow, where the woman behind the counter has a much lesser need: she is just there doing her job. That is, until Macon says something that clearly gets her attention, and suddenly gives her an entirely new objective:

> "Please," Macon said. "I'm about to catch a plane. I'm leaving for a week, and I don't have a soul to look after him. I'm desperate, I tell you."
>
> From the glance she shot at him, he sensed he had surprised her in some way.

"Can't you leave him home with your wife?"
she asked.

He wondered how on earth her mind
worked.

"If I could do that," he said, "why
would I be standing here?"

"Oh," she said. "You're not married?"

"Well, I am, but she's... living elsewhere. They don't allow pets."

"Oh."

She came out from behind the counter.
She was wearing very short red shorts; her
legs were like sticks. "I'm a divorsy myself,"
she said. "I know what you're going
through."

If we "turn down the sound" on this scene we see
that the information that Macon has handed Muriel—that
he's not living with his wife—has suddenly "upped" the
stakes for her: she actually comes out from behind the
counter. Although Macon is still on task to accomplish his
objective, Muriel's now been handed a strong want of her
own, to which Macon remains oblivious:

"So will you keep him?" Macon said.

"Oh, I guess," she said, straightening.
"If you're desperate." She stressed the
word—fixing Macon with those small brown
eyes—as if giving it more weight than he had
intended. "Fill this out," she told him, and
she handed him a form from the stack on the
counter. "Your name and address and when
you'll be back. Don't forget to put when
you'll be back."

Macon nodded, uncapping his fountain
pen.

"I'll most likely see you again when
you come to pick him up," she said. "I mean
if you put the time of day to expect you. My
name's Muriel."

"Is this place open evenings?" Macon
asked.

"Every evening but Sundays. Till
eight."

"Oh, good."

"Muriel Pritchett," she said.

Through the repetition of her name, the hints that
she'll see him if he'll "put the time of day to expect" him,
the reader understands that Muriel hopes to see Macon
when he comes back to fetch Edward. This objective (and,
in the form of Macon's obliviousness, the obstacle) pushes
forward the next section of this lovely and most satisfying
novel.

Notice, too, that Tyler keeps the activity alive,
through the dialogue, as well as what Macon is noticing
(and not) about Muriel. Macon's objective is entirely clear,
nothing sly about it, he asks directly for what he wants.
Muriel's, on other hand, is slightly more subtle and the
dialogue reflects that—she does not ask directly for what
she wants: "May I see you again?"

IN CONCLUSION AND TO REVIEW

Perhaps the most com-
mon complaint heard from
editors and teachers is how
often scenes in stories do not
DO anything. Numerous com-
ponents go in to creating an
effective scene, but the vital
element is that a scene, to <u>be</u>

> Sometimes it's only in the
> last four lines of dialogue in
> a ten-page scene that
> something <u>happens</u>—and
> that is all that should wind
> up in your novel. Learn to
> love your delete button!
> Almost inevitably, deleting
> creates tighter prose and a
> stronger story.

a scene, must <u>move something forward</u>. No matter how superb the writing may be, if nothing is revealed, if the reader does not discover anything about character or plot or theme, it is wasted space.

While this volume does not tackle creating of story per se, bear in mind that as you come to know your characters' objectives and invent or understand their obstacles, story will form, and you will build your scenes to do the work they need to do in your story. Sometimes a scene has to be written before an objective is understood; at other times, the motivations and desires and their thwarting must be grappled with before the scene can unfold on the page. Either way, the essential building block of all stories, of whatever length, is scene. These two elements—scene and story—are vitally interconnected.

A scene is where and when something happens. A scene can be one sentence long. A scene can be an entire chapter. A scene can be narrated or summarized; a scene can be dramatized. A scene must have a beginning, a middle, and an end. Something must change in the course of it, or as a result of it. Almost always, unless it is the last scene in the story, it must launch the next scene, or the next series of scenes. If it doesn't launch the next scene directly, it must nevertheless have moved something forward in the story: an aspect of a character, or an aspect of plot.

All scenes must take place somewhere, in a setting. Usually there is activity involved. A character or two is present, sometimes many more. Those characters must WANT something. They must have objectives. And in the course of the scene those objectives are or are not met: that arc is what creates a scene. A chapter can be one scene; more often a chapter is a series of scenes that add up to some accomplishment, or a definitive lack of one, on the part of one of the characters.

Dialogue must stay with the objective or show the change in the objective. It might not express the need exactly (it often shouldn't), but the reader must have a sense that the characters are pursing their needs.

In addition to putting all this to work with the following exercises, begin to take stock of the stories and novels of others. Begin to ascertain the characters' needs, and what is in the way of their accomplishing those goals. Ask this about the book or story as a whole, and ask it about individual scenes. What are the characters' objectives? Might they resonate a character's larger need? Is an objective attained? If so, whose, and does it mean that another character's is not? What does this conflict forward in the story?

PUT IT TO WORK

12. Setting up a Scene (page 239)

3. Objectives & Obstacles (page 221)

2. Establishing Character (page 219)

11. Dialogue Without Words (page 237)

25. What Does this Scene Need to Accomplish? (page 265)

7. Metaphor *en Scene* (page 229)

13. Tell Me, then Show Me (page 241)

16. Through Opposite Eyes (Other Side of the Picture) (page 250)

CROSS-PURPOSES

In a dialogue course a few years ago, a student, Randall Buechner, came up with a useful and delightful way to remember the importance of conflicting wants.

The focus of that particular class was the idea of cross-purposes: As writers we need establish a strong need for each of the main characters in a given scene, as well as what might be in the way of a character's ability to attain that need: objectives and obstacles. We talked about how the obstacle often comes in the form of another character's need—when the two objectives are at odds, the characters are at cross-purposes. We also discussed, using lists of settings and activities and objects, how using these elements in a scene help to both focus the conflict and to reveal character.

For the next class, in response to a writing assignment, Randall brought in a scene that featured a father and a daughter: The father is a recent and unwillingly-retired professor, reluctantly living at his daughter's house. He comes to the table one night to find that instead of the usual soup and sandwiches, his daughter has uncharacteristically created an elegant dinner, setting the table with the finest silver. The father is wary: what does all this fancy stuff portend, what does his daughter want?

Amongst the details to which our attention was drawn on this elegant table was a set of salt- and pepper-shakers, two miniature sterling porpoises whose mouths turned down at the corners. So much attention was paid to this little set of frowning porpoises by the author that of course we assumed them to be highly significant. We argued: The pepper is the father? The salt the daughter? She is about to make an announcement that will shake some needed pepper into his life? She is pouring salt in the wound of his enforced retirement? The chat went on like that for a bit, but the scene accomplished other necessary work. Sense of place was successfully incorporated; the dining room and candles and the meal the daughter served were unfolded in and around the dialogue—and, at times, in and around the father's refusal to partake in the daughter's chit chat—and in the 250 words allowed for the scene, an intriguing set of objectives and obstacles was launched.

When it was Randall's turn to speak he validated our suppositions about what he was up to in the scene. When we asked what on earth the might be the significance of those little frowning porpoise-shaped salt- and pepper-shakers, he grinned and said, "Well, I was just doing what Sands keeps telling us to do: making sure there are cross porpoises in every scene."

Do you have a set of cross porpoises in your scene?

POINT OF VIEW, DIALOGUE, AND SENSE OF PLACE

Critiquing a manuscript in class one day, a student said, "I wish there were a mark we could put in the margin of a manuscript that would mean, 'I need something here. I've lost track of the narrator, the point of view, even where the characters are, and I need reminding.'"

That "mark" is often composed of the letters SOP, for *sense of place*—a quick way to communicate that something more is needed about the narrator's surroundings; something the Point of View is noticing that will keep the fictional dream alive.

Sense of Place: The phrase is often interpreted to mean literally that: "a sensory impression of the space the characters are occupying," but that's a limited understanding of the term, and limits its usefulness. In addition to the physical space in which a scene is taking place, sense of place is used to maintain a reader's sense of the action, of the characters' appearance and relation to each other, even the tone underlying the dialogue. All of these are aspects of place, of a given scene's landscape. And because they are observations that the narrator is making they also serve to keep the point of view vibrant, alive.

To be effective, that observation needs to work two ways:

→   It establishes or maintains a physical sense of the scene.

AND

→   It delivers information regarding the narrator's perspective (the point of view) <u>towards</u> that scene.

That is—and this is an important point—the reader's knowledge of the narrator is supported and expanded by WHAT and HOW that character notices. It communicates the narrator's <u>sense</u> of the scene.

In this scene from Jennifer Egan's story, "The Stylist" (from her collection, *Emerald City*), observe how we never lose track of the point of view as the dialogue unfolds. In addition, observe how our understanding of the point of view character, Bernadette, grows because of what she observes, and how she observes it.

Bernadette is the stylist for a modeling shoot; Jann is the photographer. In this scene—she's come to his hotel room—she is looking through Polaroids of the shoot earlier that day:

> "Have you ever noticed how meaningful these things can look?" she asks.
>
> Jann laughs. "Have I noticed?" he says. "It's my shot."
>
> Bernadette flips the picture back among the others. Her voice goes soft. "I meant in a general sense."

> "In a general sense," says Jann, "that's how they work."
>
> The room is filled with stale light. Bernadette goes to the bed. It's amazing, she thinks, how lust and aggravation will combine to push you toward someone. She sits on the bed and then wishes she had headed for the door. She would have liked to make him ask. He would have asked, she thinks.
>
> She stretches out beside him under the twisting fan. It reminds her of a scissors. They do not touch.

The details Egan chooses to include maintain a sense of Bernadette's "physical" surroundings (the air, the fan), which have already been established in the scene leading up to this excerpt. Here, the air is characterized as "stale," which reflects Bernadette's cynicism about the act in which she's about to engage; and the twisting fan is likened to a "scissors," another clue to her emotions: she has earlier told Jann that the hotel reminds her of one in New Orleans, where she spent her honeymoon.

This attention to the narrator's observations, her personal <u>sense</u> of the place (and place includes the setting and any characters in that setting), means that no detail is "wasted." Everything the writer includes allows the reader to stay in touch with the narrator. In addition to maintaining an effective point of view, this also engages the reader in discovering what a character wants from a given scene, and if s/he is accomplishing that want.

When a writer puts his characters into conversation, at times a "tape recorder" seems to replace the "camera" (that sophisticated and powerful camera of point of view, which records more than the aural and visual of a given scene). When this tape recorder replaces the camera, the reader's feeling of intimacy with the narrator falls away. The reader is left to figure out for himself, or to imagine, the characters' possible reactions to what's being said in the scene. The reader also has to invent the possible actions or gestures that might be going on during or between the lines of dialogue. Managed skillfully, this can be effective, but too often it is confusing. Again, see how Egan handles this as the conversation, after Jann and Bernadette have made love, continues:

> They lie in silence. Bernadette decides she will go back to her own room. Conversation is meant to get you somewhere, and she and Jann have already been and gone.
>
> "You know," he says, "it's hard to picture you married."
>
> "I hardly was. It lasted a minute."
>
> "How did it end?"
>
> "Christ!" she says. "What have I started here?
>
> "Tell me."
>
> She narrows her eyes and sits up. With her toes she searches the floor for her sandals.
>
> "You can't answer a simple question," says Jann. "Can you?"
>
> Bernadette touches her knuckles to her lips. The door is ten feet from the bed. She wishes she were dressed.
>
> "I got restless," she says.
>
> "Restless," says Jann.
>
> "You know—restless? I kept thinking how many places there were."
>
> Jann laughs. "I guess you picked the right life."

"I guess so," says Bernadette. She fumbles for her lighter. "You know," she says, "you ask too many questions."

She lights a cigarette and smokes it lavishly...

As Egan keeps the camera of Bernadette's point of view alive, we see Bernadette's desire to leave, and her ambivalence about actually doing so. Each of the selected details accomplishes something: forwarding a piece of characterization and underscoring important information already presented in the story.

She lies back down, her body facing Jann's. His shoulder smells faintly sweet, like beeswax. She places her palm on his stomach, but when she tries to move her hand, Jann covers it with his own.

"Of all those places you've been," he says, "which was your favorite?"

Bernadette sighs. She is tired of questions. Strangely, she cannot remember anyone having asked her this one before. Is that possible? she wonders. Surely someone asked, surely she had some answer. She tries again to move her hand. Jann holds it still.

"I liked them all," she says.

"Bullshit."

She feels a surge of regret at finding herself still here, at getting caught in this discussion. Jann moves her hand from his stomach to his chest. The skin is warmer there, close to the bone. She can feel the beating heart.

"There must be one that stands out," he says.

Bernadette hesitates.

"New Orleans," she says. "My honey-moon."

It is the only place she can think of. She feels suddenly that she might begin to cry.

Jann lets her hand go. He turns on his side so they are facing each other. Their hips touch.

"It must be quite a place." His voice is gentle now.

Bernadette moves against him. She cannot stop herself. Jann takes her head in his hands and makes her look at him. "Hey," he says, "what does this remind you of?"

He is playful, teasing. A thin silver chain encircles his neck.

"Nothing," she says. Something is caught in her throat.

By letting the reader know what and how Bernadette observes, Egan deepens our understanding of Bernadette. And all of it is shown to the reader, not told to us: we get to reach in and figure out for ourselves what she's gone through.

And—vital point—we get to know how Bernadette is CHANGING. Her cynicism at the beginning of the scene has been replaced with an ability to "feel the beating heart," and even a desire to cry. And she notices the silver chain around Jann's neck, a signal filled with potency, communicating a kind of dependability: in the surface-celebrating, youth-adoring, ever-changing world of fashion, here is someone with a past, someone who is not afraid to wear a badge of connection.

As the narrative unfolds, these and other observations and details gather power and momentum. Through a deft combination of point of view and sense of place, Egan allows us to clearly visualize the various settings of "The Stylist"; in addition, we are given the gift of Bernadette's emotional landscape.

PUT IT TO WORK

EXERCISES:

See "Dialogue Pitfalls and Helpful Hints."

12. Setting up a Scene (page 239)
     and / or
21. Point of View, Dialogue & Sense of Place (page 259)
22. Three Lines of Dialogue (page 261)
25. What Does This Scene Need to Accomplish? (page 265)

With these ideas in mind, go back and take another look at exercises such as:

7.   Metaphor *en Scene* (page 229)
13. Tell Me, then Show Me (page 241)
15. Through Close Eyes (page 247)
16. Through Opposite Eyes (Other side of the Picture) (page 250)

SOME DIALOGUE PITFALLS
AND HELPFUL HINTS

1)   NO REASON FOR DIALOGUE

Sometimes a scene isn't really ABOUT anything. The characters talk but nothing actually gets accomplished. Nothing is pushed forward.

Solution: Be sure you know what the scene needs to accomplish. Sometimes this only happens as we work on a scene. It will help to begin with some idea of what a scene needs to encompass, at least in terms of character and plot. What does the scene need to push forward in terms of the story? The characters?

As you start work on a scene be sure at least one character wants something. Create tension. Some sort of cross-purpose. Argument.

→   Characters in a scene have opposite needs.

→   Characters share an intense need that is op-
       posed by some exterior force, or by another
       character(s).

→   One character wants one thing and another
       character wants something else that isn't in
       opposition but nevertheless creates conflict.

2)   UNANCHORED SPEAKERS

Two people are talking to each other, but we don't
know where they are. They are also not doing anything. As
a result, we also often get confused as to who's who.

Solution: Sense of Place (SOP): Be sure your scene
takes place somewhere, and be sure you establish a sense
of that environment, at or towards the beginning of the
scene.

In addition, you might choose to maintain the setting and activity as the scene unfolds, with references to
surroundings or objects, or even to the other character;
people after all, are a part of "place."

3)   ATTRIBUTION PROBLEMS

A)   NO ATTRIBUTIONS AT ALL

We could be reading a play without any stage direc-
tions (similar to Pitfall #1).

This is often a stylistic choice, and can be used very
effectively (as it was by Hemingway in "Hills Like White
Elephants"). It takes skill to individualize the voices of the
characters and their respective concerns and objectives
need to be at odds, so that who is saying what remains
clear.

Solution: Distinct character voices and/or objectives, and/or SOP.

B)   AN OVERUSE OF *SAID*

This is often a stylistic choice, and can be effective; many writers use "said" almost every line, and it can virtually disappear.

But it can also get in the way.

Solution: Put characters in action.

Replace "said" with something they are doing.

C)   REPLACING "SAID" WITH OTHER "TALKING" VERBS

This can be humorous rather than helpful:

> "Are you going to the store?" asked Joan.
> "I am," replied Claire.
> "Remember to get milk this time?!" Joan demanded.
> "Certainly," assured Claire. "Do we still need bread as well?" she queried.
> "Bread and milk and eggs, the staples," retorted Joan.
> "That's what I'll buy, then," Claire declared.

You get the point. Of course, each of these verbs can be useful and specific. But when a writer uses words such as commented, replied, informed, announced, responded, declared, added, answered, rejoined, retorted, remarked, shouted, screamed, cried, etc. to replace "said," it usually means not enough attention has been paid to the line of dialogue itself (which should BE a comment, or a rejoinder, or a shout), or characterization is not clear, or—again—sense of place is lacking.

Solution: Avoid an overuse or dependency on verbs. Instead, use effective dialogue to show the needed verb, or an action (what a character is doing) to reveal character and tone.

Use "said," and/or the solution suggested for #2b.

D) USING SAID AND/OR OTHER "TALKING VERBS" + AN ADVERB

> he responded, casually
>
> she screamed, angrily
>
> he commented, wryly
>
> he remarked, offhandedly
>
> she asked, interrogatively

Solution: The dialogue itself is the solution: the comment needs to SHOW the "wry"; the remark needs to BE "offhand"; the words screamed need to REVEAL the anger.

Again, putting the characters into action as they speak will help the reader see these things even more clearly: shrugging or lighting a cigarette could show the casual, throwing an ashtray could reveal the anger.

Note: Unless lack of attribution is a stylistic choice, the above pitfalls often come about because the "camera" —the point of view on the scene— has been turned off or forgotten, and all that is running is a usually much less interesting "tape recorder."

4)   A MISUNDERSTANDING OF WHAT COMPRISES "REALISTIC" DIALOGUE

> "Well, uh..." Norm said, as he sipped his coffee. "Good morning, Nancy, ummm. How are you?"
>
> "Well, Norm, ah..." Nancy put her paper cup under the blue faucet of the water

cooler, lifted it to her lips and sipped. "I'm, uh, better.... I guess... umm. And you?"

When a writer chooses to include every *Well, um, er, uh, ah*, a simple greeting gets charged with all kinds of other possible meanings: Are Norm and Nancy in love with each other? Is there some secret between them?

This can also include an overuse of slang or colloquialisms. This gets into Point of View and Voice.

Solution: Be sure you know <u>what the scene is about</u> and delete everything that isn't needed to reveal the tension in the scene or to characterize your speakers. For instance, if you're trying to establish Norm's shyness or lack of assertiveness, use words like "umm" sparingly, and SHOW Norm's character through action (or inaction) in a scene.

5)   DIALECT OVER-EMPHASIS

Sometimes a writer overuses punctuation and odd spellings to "show" how something is pronounced. Alice Walker did it effectively in *The Color Purple*, but most of the time it just gets in the way of meaning, and can even be almost impossible to read.

Solution: Rely on rhythm and syntax rather than punctuation and spelling.

6)   AN OVER-USE OF NAMES IN DIALOGUE

"Hey, Tim, you got that phone line rigged up yet?"

"No, Steve. The wire was the wrong size. I had to reorder."

"What a bummer, Tim. When's it due in?"

"They said tomorrow. What a hassle, eh, Steve?"

"I'll say, Tim. When we thought it'd be done by now."

Solution: Again, put them in action. Let us SEE them clearly, and we'll know which is Tim and which is Steve.

Better yet, make one of them clearly a hard worker and one a sluffer—and maintain their characterization through the lines they are given to say. And/or find a bigger problem they have to solve; and/or establish a larger conflict they have with each other.

7)   DIALOGUE AS EXPOSITION

With Dialogue as Exposition—with Exposition in general, ask yourself:

→   Does the Reader need to know this now?

and

→   Does the Reader need to know this yet?

—and

→   Does the Reader need to know this at all?

The answer, disconcertingly often, is "no."

John hugged Mary as she came through the door. "I'm so sorry, Mary. Who could have known that the stroke, which occurred three months ago, would have required your uncle to go into the hospital and stay there and that you've had to visit him every day for the last month?"

Mary shrugged her way out of her ragged, patched coat. "Isn't it true, John? And in the meantime we've also had to be over at his house going through his papers, and deciding what to do about the inheritance. Oh, that chicken smells so good! You've done my favorite recipe, the one with rosemary; you are the most perfect househusband, and our marriage is so blessed. Do you think we should just pull the plug on Uncle, and take all the money ourselves?"

OR

"What do you have in that suitcase, Charlie?"

"Nothing much, Dad. I'll just zip it closed, here. This train we're on is rocking, so I'm a little off balance, see."

"Yeah, Charlie. I'm having to grip this bar to keep upright myself. Did you know— that was your grandmother's suitcase. It's more than sixty years old. Look at all those decals from the foreign countries she visited on her honeymoon. Rome, Paris, Madrid."

"Wow, Dad, that's really moving. Give me your handkerchief, would you, and let me wipe these tears that are flowing freely out of my eyes."

"Yeah, well, Charlie, take it. I don't want to sound too gruff here, but your grandmother was quite a woman. Blow your nose, that's the way, and let's sit down here on these seats that face one another and look out at the French countryside we're traveling through while I tell you about her."

"Okay, Dad. I'm sitting now. I've wiped my eyes. Look at that spotted cow! And that quaintly timbered barn! Oh, I'm sorry, Dad, don't look so disapproving with your brows

all drawn down like that. Go on. I'm ready to
hear all about her."

Solution: In Mary and John's case these two paragraphs seem to hold the précis for the entire novel. A solution might be to start with a different scene altogether:
when the Uncle first took sick, or Mary going through Uncle's papers, or John bringing Mary some food or a
toothbrush at the hospital, delivering information through
inference, trusting the reader to read between action and
lines of dialogue.

Dad and Charlie are more absurd, of course, although I have seen exactly this kind of writing in early
manuscripts—it's as if the author forgets that action and
description are available and must rely only on dialogue.
Here again, much could be solved by selecting a point of
view, making sure we're in a setting, and letting us see
through that specific pair of eyes/perceptions.

PUT IT TO WORK

EXERCISES:

11. Dialogue Without Words (page 237)

22. Three Lines of Dialogue (page 261)

21. Point of View, Dialogue, & Sense of Place
     (page 259)

24. Dialogue: Some Special Cases (page 263)

23. Dialogue: Employing Syntax and Vocabulary
     (page 262)

PUT IT TO WORK:

THE EXERCISES

**AS YOU PUT IT TO WORK,
PLEASE KEEP THE FOLLOWING IN MIND.**

Regarding the writing that emerges as a result of these exercises: There is no "right" or "wrong." There is more effective and less effective, but no "incorrect."

Frustrating though it may be, limit your word-count to those suggested at the bottom of each exercise. This is especially true if you are putting it to work in a group. The delete button is your friend. Almost always, as you work within the word limit, you will gain lessons in what is essential and what is not. If you are inspired to write more, great—but, if in a group, choose salient paragraphs to share with the class, and if working on your own, strive to work within the focus of the particular exercise.

You will often be tempted to create a scene out of these exercises with a beginning, middle and end. This is a great ambition, but often difficult within the word count prescribed. Bear in mind that you might simply advance one or two things about a character. What you work on here does not need to reveal everything about your character to your reader. In fact, ideally, it should not. Ideally it will whet your reader's appetite and, one hopes, your own as well.

Very important: <u>Do not use these exercises to re-work a scene you've already written</u>.

If you want to work on a scene or a character you have in mind, terrific. Or feel free to rewrite—<u>but from scratch</u>—a scene you've already composed. What I don't want you to do is to try to apply these exercises to a scene you've already put on a page. Start fresh, so you get the full benefit of what the exercise asks you to examine.

Particular exercises will be useful in exploring troublesome scenes in a piece you're currently writing. However, no matter how much you're tempted to apply the ideas to an already-written scene, <u>start anew</u>. Otherwise the benefits of putting it to work may escape you.

When you remember to do so, observe yourself at work. What can attention to your own process tell you?

If you enjoy doing one exercise more than another, try to determine, why? What challenges you? What makes you feel nervous, inept? What makes you feel confident? You might begin to watch, for example, how you already do, or do not, weave autobiography into your fiction. Or, observe which of the various points of view make you feel most "at home" and what happens when you are asked to write something in an altogether different point of view.

This attention to your own process might be awkward at first, but it will begin to teach you how you write and—importantly—how to *improve* what you write.

And have fun.

1

LISTS OF THREE

IMPLICATION & INFERENCE

Note: Below are some examples; invent your own.

List three settings (if you like, include place and time):

→   A theatre an hour after the show has ended.

→   The built-in barbecue in the back yard at the Smythe's house; it is a little after five.

→   The dining room in a medieval castle; this scene might take place in 2001 — or in 1210.

List three activities (these may or may not have anything to do with your previous list; you may or may not include who is doing the activity):

→   Betty mends a cracked bowl as Sam looks on

→   Making martinis

→   A teenager and a middle-aged man snowboarding

LIST THREE OBJECTS:

→   Needle and red thread

→ Glue

→ Pruning shears

List three character names (who are they? why might you name them this way?):

→ <u>Bud</u>: he drinks Mickeys and knits socks for those who have been diagnosed HIV positive; he's your "average joe"; but is he?

→ <u>Minerva</u>: dresses in black; is a Scorpio and not everyone likes her; she's a little "witchy."

→ <u>Matilda</u>: the five-year-old child of a troubled couple who hope that their expectations for a happy, "old-fashioned" life will somehow be manifested in their daughter.

Now: jot a few notes about what you might be able to <u>imply</u> with these items. What might you want a reader to infer, and how might you "shape" that inference?

Much depends on context and specific description; those ideas might be part of these notes.

There is no need to write anything formal; the exercise is to ask yourself how places and activities, objects and character names, can help shape a reader's sense of your characters.

How you can employ them <u>purposefully</u>, to carry more meaning than at first they appear to do? How might there be a shift in meaning by how and where you put them to use?

2

ESTABLISHING CHARACTER

REVEAL A CHARACTER IN A <u>PLACE</u> (SETTING), <u>DOING</u> SOMETHING (ACTIVITY), AND/OR <u>USING</u> SOMETHING (OBJECT).

The idea is to select and utilize setting, activity, and/or objects so that your reader discovers — because you show them, rather then tell them — something essential about the nature of your character. Explore what can be communicated simply through action/activity and setting.

<u>Do not use the character talking to herself</u>. The exercise is to have setting and action, not something your character says aloud, communicate information to the reader.

<u>Do not rely on inner thought</u>: Similarly, do not rely on what your character may be thinking to communicate with the reader. Your character can reflect on something that reveals an aspect of his nature; what I don't want is this: "Joe felt so bad. His wife had walked out on him last night. Of course the hangover didn't help. He wished to God he hadn't spent last night consuming the better part of a bottle of Glenlivet." Much of what is here revealed through inner thought can be revealed through effective choice of setting (bar, hotel room) and activity/objects (emptying a shot glass, a hot shower.) The reader might not get everything, but they will get a lot.

Concentrate on sense of place: get your reader to see, hear, feel the setting and the activity you're creating. Use how the character interacts with those things to show that, say, Joe is miserable—it is even possible to communicate, without telling us, that he no longer has a wife.

POSSIBLE WAYS TO APPROACH THIS EXERCISE:

(a) You might take a character from a story or novel (not necessarily your "main" character, or even a point of view character). Make it your objective to reveal something to the reader about them by where we find them and what they are doing.

(b) Use your Lists of Three: You might start with a setting and see if a character comes to you out of the description you create—such as by asking yourself who is it that is looking at a particular setting may help you find the character (an effective way to develop a point of view).

(c) You might start with an activity and see what sort of person might be involved.

However you approach it, let us discover something about a character by <u>where</u> we find them (setting) and <u>what</u> they are doing (activity, object).

250 words.

3

OBJECTIVES & OBSTACLES

PART ONE

Apply the first five questions to a scene you are creating and discuss the following for at least two of your characters:

PART TWO

Use all the questions to discuss the larger needs of your characters:

→ What does your character want, need? (Do you feel "want" and "need" are different? If so, discuss.) <u>Objective</u>.

→ How is she/he going about getting what she/he wants or needs?

→ What's in the way of getting what s/he wants/needs? <u>Obstacle</u>.

→ Could you—or do you feel a need to—make either the objective or the obstacle stronger/higher? Why? How?

→ Make a list of some ways in which your character will go about getting what s/he wants.

→   Do these make you imagine some encounters
     or conversations your character might have?
     Discuss.

→   What might be some smaller objectives your
     character might strive to accomplish on the
     way to accomplishing the big one?

PART THREE

→   Do these questions make you want to change
     anything about how you're proceeding with
     your story or novel? Describe.

4

Searching for Significance

As you go about your day, take in the settings in which you find yourself, the activities in which you and others engage, and the objects that are handled. If you don't already do this—and some of you no doubt do—look for meaning in these things. If you found them in a story, what might be revealed?

Listen and look for how our culture puts simile and metaphor to work:

→ Tune your radio to a pop station and listen to song lyrics. Note down effective or amusing uses of metaphor and simile.

→ Look at headlines; sports pages are often fun places to begin: see how nouns and verbs are put together to create pictures for the reader.

→ Take a look at advertisements—billboards, radio ads, television ads, ads in magazines... What do they visually do? Do they force the viewer to put two unlike things together? Is a picture influenced by the text printed on the page with it? Underscored? Changed?

→   Start noting especially good uses of figures of speech and language in magazine articles and books.

→   Similarly, take a look at and examine the titles of some favorite books and stories and songs and plays and movies: how are they significant? How do they effectively capture or illuminate what's in the piece of art?

Now: back to your own movements through life: Start making lists: of your actions and the activities of those around you (sweeping up the cat litter in the laundry room, staking a tomato, peeling 25 cloves of garlic). Take a look at where things happen (playground, café, riverbank, fire escape). List some objects (a postage stamp, scissors, an egg, an address book). Think about the situation in which you find them: what might they convey, beside the literal? What might they mean if placed in a different context, or if performed by or utilized by someone else? What if one of your characters found themselves in this setting, or performing this activity?

Keeping in mind that one of the component parts of the word "significant" is SIGN—it points towards something—write up some notes about what, if anything, this exercise does for you.

5

Combining Elements

Pull out your Lists of Three. Combine at least three of those elements into a short scene in which you reveal a single character in action. If you use dialogue at all, keep it minimal. The focus here is on characterization.

For instance: I might try putting both Minerva and Matilda into a theatre an hour after a show has ended. Minerva is making martinis for some cast members while her daughter Matilda plays in the aisles. I might try to fit in glue (repairing the stem of a broken glass); or the pruning shears. Suddenly I realize these are a "prop" from the show and are being played with by Matilda in a dangerous and horrifying fashion: this helps me reveal that Minerva is not talking good care of her daughter.

Or: I might try to put Bud, who is, I realize as I write, HIV positive, in that medieval castle, using the needle and thread (which he always carries with him) to repair a ancient tapestry he has inadvertently torn. Perhaps as a result of looking closely at the tapestry he finds himself back in time, where there is a very different sort of plague raging—and I can use both my time periods.

So: **Reveal a character in a <u>place</u> (setting), <u>doing</u> something (activity/object), and/or <u>using</u> something (object/prop).**

The idea is to select and utilize setting, activity, and/or objects to imply information: your reader discovers information because you show them, rather then tell them something about your character.

Keep it active; try not to rely on inner thought or dialogue to reveal your character to us; let us discover something essential about their nature by your thoughtful choice of where we find them and what they are doing.

250 words.

6

CHECKLIST FOR A SCENE

→ Where is the scene set? Does the setting convey some information about at least one of the characters?

→ What activity might at least one character be engaged in that might reveal to the reader something specific about them?

→ What objects, or "props," might your characters handle? Are these items the most specific, most "telling" objects available in the setting or by the activity? Could they be interpreted on metaphoric or symbolic levels?

→ What do each of the characters in the scene want? What is in the way of getting what they want?

→ Explore the idea of expressing your characters' emotional states by how they move about the space, engage in the activity, use the objects.

→ Employ dialogue wisely. Make sure each character speaks distinctly—by which I mean uniquely—and that what they say lets the reader know something specific. Avoid adverbs in your attributions; use action and gesture to convey tone of voice and attitude.

→   What is the source of light in the setting? Are there sounds? Aromas? Use sensory perceptions as a way to reveal point of view and the setting.

→   At the same time, remember that each detail needs to contribute something, needs to reveal something about character or objective/ obstacle (plot), or theme.

7

METAPHOR *EN SCENE*

Using your lists as a springboard (but do not feel confined by them if other ideas come to mind), write a scene involving two characters.

Note: the scene has to accomplish something: one character wants something and does or does not get it.

Concentrate on establishing a setting that conveys something specific about your character(s). Find an activity that shows the reader something about his or her nature. If you draw our attention to objects, see if they, too, can convey something specific about your characters.

If you find that characters' names serve you in some fashion, incorporate those as well.

Use dialogue minimally—do not rely on it to "tell" the reader what is going on in the scene. Let the setting and activity do as much work as possible.

Similarly, try not to rely on inner thought to reveal your character to us; let us discover something about them by a thoughtful choice of where we find them and what they are doing.

Along the way, employ one simile and small-m metaphor, including some interesting, active verbs.

300 words.

8

MY TWO GRANDMOTHERS

→   First: Write a character description of a person you know well. Include detail. Make it
lively. Make it your objective to let your
reader know this person as well as possible in
the short space allowed, This means that your
description will probably include what they
look like, and perhaps a telling incident in
which they were involved. **250 words.**

→   Second: Write a description of a person with
the same relationship to you, but this time *invent* the character. Again, you will probably
want to describe them physically and invent
actions that will reveal them clearly to your
readers. Use detail. **250 words.**

That is, write two one-page, 250-word pieces enti-
tled, "My Grandmother" or "My Best Friend." My Boss." "My
Little Sister." They may certainly have different names, but
the relationship to you is the same. One of these descriptions is of the *real* person, whom you know. The other
description is of a *fictional* character.

My grandma Rosie is somebody you
might read about in a fairy tale: she really is
almost as round as she is tall; her cheeks are
often red, she wears her hair curled like a

white rope on top of her head. And she wears
wire spectacles. But she has a temper. Once,
when grandfather came in late for supper,
she yanked off one of her low-heeled shoes
and hurled it at him across the room. It
would have hit him, but he ducked. It
bounced off the wall and fell onto artificial
fruits in the bowl on the coffee table. He
brought her the shoe, which she slipped back
on and then commanded us to use our forks
for the purpose God made them, not hanging
out in front of our mouths like we expected
Manna to fall into them from Heaven.

All I know of my grandmother Harriet
are stories I've been told by my mother,
though I've seen photographs of her: slender
and doe-eyed, hair curled tight against her
head. She died on my mother's fifth birthday,
so my memories of her are my mother's
memories: Mother remembers her laughing.
She remembers parties, with brightly-lit Chinese lanterns strung across the lawn. She
remembers the sound of cast iron curtain
hooks sliding against a cast iron curtain rod,
as drapes were opened or shut. She remembers a summer night when she was sleeping
on the screened-in sleeping porch and her
mother came running up from a midnight
swim in the Delta to check on her, leaning
over her crib, warm drops of water falling
from her mother's face onto her own.

Ideally, a reader will have a hard time figuring out
which one of these descriptions is your invented aunt,

mother, boss, etc., and which is the real one—try to keep them guessing.

    NOTE: You can write about the invented person as yourself. Or you can create someone, a persona, and write about the invented person from that perspective—as if you are an actor, adopting a role, and improvising a monologue about this person in your invented life. Stay aware of how this might alter the voice, the description, the language and vocabulary you use— do they change as you write one, then the other of these descriptions?

    Stay aware of point of view in other ways as well. For instance, you will probably write about the "real" character in First Person, but might be tempted to write about the invented one in Third. Make a choice, and be consistent.

    And without letting it get in your way, try to stay aware of your responses to your own process as you work on this:

    →   Is it hard or easy to stick to only what really happened?

    →   Is it surprisingly easy or is it difficult to invent circumstances?

    →   Is it fun to write about someone you know well and make it sound "fictional?"

    →   Is it more fun to invent someone entirely new? To "be" someone different than yourself as you write about someone you're inventing?

    →   Did this exercise make you aware that you might be creating a narrator, a persona, which is not you? Is this point of view one you would like to explore more deeply?

250 words for each description.

9

I Still Believe in Unicorns

Recall an incident that happened to you or to someone you know that contains a fragment of conversation you particularly remember.

→   Write that incident, including the fragment of conversation, **keeping as close to the actual incident as you can.** (You might, of course, have all kinds of other dialogue around the actual fragment you intend to use.) Include *where* you were (place) and *what* you were doing (activity). Make it as descriptive and powerful as possible, but discipline yourself to stick to the actual details of the actual incident. **250 words.**

→   Then, taking that same fragment of conversation, write **an entirely invented scene** that contains that piece of dialogue. Surround it with invented action and fictional conversation. That is, avoid simply writing the scene using people similar to yourself, in similar circumstances: invent new circumstances in which this piece of dialogue still makes sense—makes sense in an entirely new way. **250 words.**

Example: a student who works as a hospice nurse wrote a piece in which she is reading a story about unicorns and princesses to her daughter at bedtime. As she hugs her daughter goodnight, the girl says, "I still believe in unicorns."

For the second half of the assignment the student used her experience with hospice: as a nurse removes a tray of untouched food and changes the bed sheets of a man with AIDS, the two speak of the need to keep faith and hope alive when one knows one is dying, and he tells her, "I still believe in unicorns."

We had a hard time guessing which one of these was the real incident (the daughter) and which fictional. She used first-person point of view in each one, and selected effective detail to make readers feel that they were in the room with these characters.

As you work on this, and without letting it get in your way, try to stay aware of your response to your process:

→ Does folding what really happened into what might have happened come easily?

→ Is it hard or is it easy to stick to only what really happened?

→ Is it easy or is it difficult to invent circumstances? Dialogue? Characters? Etc.

→ Does the point of view change when you move to an invented scene? Is a person similar to you a character in the scene? Is the narrator similar to you? Quite dissimilar?

→ Were you able to stay aware of and be consistent in the point of view you chose?

250 words for each incident.

10

SEEING THROUGH OTHER EYES
OR
GETTING SOME PERSPECTIVE

NOTE: Use this to see what it feels like to occupy another character in your story or novel. You can also use it as a way to begin to get to know, or to know more deeply, some of your characters.

Also useful as a step towards writing "Through Eyes That Slide" or for "Through Omniscient Eyes."

Select three characters that know your point of view character.

From each point of view:

In 50-150 words, a paragraph or two, have each one express his or her opinion about your character.

→ Use First Person for at least one.

→ Use Third Person for at least one.

In either case, explore the idea of "voice."

If you like, after reading "When the Narrator has Distance," try a distant or omniscient narrator that observes and comments on your character.

For example, if Mark Twain were to try this exercise he might write about Huck

(a)   from the perspective of Jim, the runaway
         slave, in first person

(b)   using the point of view of Aunt Polly in
         third, and

(c)   from the perspective of the river, or from
         the perspective of some wide-angle lens, for
         an omniscient take on an aspect of Huck's
         adventures or character.

If J.D. Salinger were to try it, he might describe Holden Caulfield:

(a)   in the outraged or worried first person per-
         spective of one of his teachers

(b)   from the third person perspective of his sis-
         ter, Phoebe

(c)   from his father's point of view, in either
         first or third, and/or

(d)   from the perspective of the school as a
         whole.

50 – 150 words each.

11

DIALOGUE WITHOUT WORDS

For a revealing exercise in writing dialogue, don't use any dialogue.

Reveal Character A in a <u>place</u> (setting) <u>doing</u> something (activity). Character B might already be in the scene, or B might enter. Either way, B, who has an ISSUE she or he wants to address, interrupts or ignores or engages or irritates A because A also has an objective—something s/he needs or is trying to accomplish.

Example: Rick is in his study, installing a new memory chip in his computer. He needs it because his computer keeps crashing and he has a major project that has to be completed by tomorrow. His estranged wife, Miranda, enters, unannounced and unwelcome, wanting half of the $200 he promised would be his share when they splurged on a "we-can-make-this-work" dinner three months ago. Perhaps we only we see the beginning of this scene, as Rick is at work on the innards of his computer, and Miranda enters, waving a receipt.

Or: we see two people in bed, after making love, and the actions they are given—lighting a cigarette, a certain kind of embrace, rising to open a window or put on a nightgown—lets the reader know the essence of what this moment is for them.

Part of the idea is to select and utilize setting & activity so that your reader discovers—because you show them, rather then tell them—something essential about at least one, if not both, of your characters.

Do not use dialogue. The exercise is to have setting and action, not something your characters say, communicate to the reader. This may be frustrating, and give you all kinds of ideas about what you WILL have them say to each other when you have a chance. Do not tell us what they would be saying. Part of the effort is to explore how we communicate without words.

Similarly, avoid "expositiony" inner thought. Inner monologue is a method, which I don't want you to employ here, of telling rather than showing your reader the content of a scene.

SO: Using no dialogue, let us discover something about the relationship between two characters by where we find them and what they are doing, and how they may respond to one another.

300 words.

12

SETTING UP A SCENE

Establish why the scene needs to take place: your objective as an author: It will forward x in the plot, it will introduce this character, it will complicate this relationship... that sort of thing. This should include issues of plot that you want to forward, as well as character development (what more can the reader discover, about each one, no matter how ancillary, in the course of this scene), as well as introducing or continuing the reader's engagement with and knowledge of the setting.

(For our purposes, select a scene with only two or three characters. Later, you can apply these principles to a scene inhabited by more characters.)

Establish what's at stake: what does each character want?

Establish where the scene is set, and why. Select an activity that reveals something about at least one of your characters and/or the tension in the scene.

Clarify for yourself these things:

→   Why the scene needs to take place.

→   What each character wants.

→   What is in the way of getting what they want.

→   Ponder the idea of "Turning down the Sound."

Remember that one person's objective may change when another person enters or when they say or ask something that may change the want or the stakes.

SO: In a paragraph or two or three, sketch out what the scene, were you to write it, needs to reveal.

Now: Write the scene.

350 words.

13

TELL ME, THEN SHOW ME

(DO BOTH PARTS OF THIS EXERCISE)

PART ONE: "TELL ME" (NARRATIVE)

Imagine a scene that involves two, nor more than three, characters, at least one of whom has something they want (an objective) and something in the way of getting that want (an obstacle). (See "Setting up a Scene.") Write a narrative sentence to describe it, such as: "When Joe dropped by Velma's house that day he fully expected her to agree to the idea of a divorce; after all, hadn't they been living separately for almost a year?" (Do not use this one—invent your own.)

In your narrative sentence, 15-50 words, give us a summary of what the scene is "about." Make sure there is tension; at least one of the characters has a strong need. There is something in the way of that need. The need gets met or it does not.

→   A character wants something he can't have: Joe wants a divorce, but Velma, who has not been a practicing Catholic in years, has suddenly decided she can't thwart her faith.

→   A character wants something that is thwarted—this can be unconscious (or seemingly unconscious)—by the needs of the other character: Joe wants to ask for a divorce, but he walks into a fight between Velma and their daughter, which he has to referee. OR Joe wants a divorce, but Velma's beloved cat has just been run over. OR Joe wants a divorce, but as he begins the conversation, Velma (who may know what is coming) asks him if he would please just take a look at the broken garbage disposal; she's *desperate*. OR, Joe wants a divorce but is also susceptible to Velma's sexuality, and she knows it and puts it to work.

→   A character wants something and gets it, perhaps in an unexpected way: Joe wants a divorce; when he finally works up his nerve to ask for one, he finds Velma upstairs, in bed with his old friend Johnny.

Make sure it's narrative—you're purposefully <u>telling</u> the reader what is going on in the scene, as well as any other levels you may be implying.

If you are working with a group, do not share this part, "Tell Me," until after your dramatization, "Show Me," has been discussed; then see if what the group "got" is what you intended.

Narrative sentence: 15 - 50 words.

PART TWO: "SHOW ME" (DRAMATIZATION)

Write the <u>dramatized</u> version of your narrative sentence. That is, reveal to your reader, in scene, the information contained in your summary.

<u>Show</u> rather than tell the reader what tension exists. (It does not necessarily need to be a fight.)

Be sure to include Sense of Place (it might help to use the idea of "turning down the sound"):

Where are your characters: how can your setting help reveal something about the nature of the argument? How might the character(s)' activity/ies be used to convey characterization, as well as tension?

How might you have them use objects to convey the tone of what they are saying?

What actions and gestures might you incorporate to help reveal what's going on in the scene?

Avoid dialogue pitfalls:

→   If your characters speak (silence can be pow-
     erful) to one another, explore what they don't
     say, or what they say instead of what they
     want to say.

→   See what happens if none of your dialogue di-
     rectly addresses the conflict. Maybe the dia-
     logue says one thing and the action in the
     scene quite another.

Avoid adverbs in the attributions. Instead, use action (such as how they handle their "props," how they move about the space or use a gesture) to convey tone of voice and attitude.

Try to include a few sensory perceptions.

At the same time remember that each detail needs to contribute something. It is included in order to reveal something to the reader. That is, in fifteen to fifty words write a narrative or summary sentence and then dramatize the scene you have described.

Note: When you have finished the dramatization, be sure it "matches" your narrative sentence. You may need to rewrite your narrative so it reflects what you have actually dramatized.

Dramatization: 350 - 500 words.

Further Note: This exercise is useful when you begin to recognize a series of scenes you need to write for your story. You can summarize them quickly, and then come back to actually create them as scenes.

14

THE LOOP

Using as a leaping-off point an exercise such as "Tell Me, Then Show Me" or a scene from your current manuscript, compose an *Expanded Narrative*, or a "Loop."

Note: Be sure you have a sense of what it is you think the reader needs to know as a result of this movement back in time, or into your character's thought-processes. Something significant needs to be pushed forward; there is a purpose to this scene as much as there is to any other you include in your story. (It is also a great way to get to know your characters, and can be deleted, later).

→   **ground** your reader in the present tense of the scene. This could be:

Something about the setting: a sensory perception (sight, sound, smell, taste, feeling—tactile or emotional);

→   An object ("prop");

→   An activity.

Then take us on a loop through the mind/memory of your point-of-view character. As you move back in time, or into a thought process, try to avoid phrases such as, "He remembered," and, similarly, when you return, phrases such as, "Now, as he..."

Your character might reflect on something germane to the scene he's just "left," or to a relationship; it can be a flashback that will be revealing in some way about an is-sue—overtly addressed or not—raised in or by that scene.

Again: Be sure the information contained in the loop contributes in some way to the character, his history, what's at stake between him and another person in the scene, or something that is influencing his behavior in some way; whatever it is, the loop needs to further our understanding about an issue raised in and by the scene out of which it arises, and/or in your story as a whole.

Be sure to return us to the scene and to the estab-lished setting, sensory perception, object, and/or activity.

**350 words,
including getting into and coming out of the loop.**

15

THROUGH CLOSE EYES

(DO BOTH PARTS OF THIS EXERCISE)

PART ONE

Using a **first-**person point of view, write a scene that includes at least two people and some form of conflict. (See "Objectives and Obstacles.")

The conflict does not have to be violent, nor does it need to be articulated. Explore showing, rather than telling, the tension in the scene.

You might try occupying a viewpoint—a character— other than your own; try on a persona, as an actor might. If you are a woman in your forties who works in a medical facility, try writing from the perspective of a teenager who works as a busboy.

Explore the idea of a **voice** (one of the strengths of First Person) that is not your own.

Explore the sorts of things this narrator would observe that you might not, and ways in which this narrator might articulate those things differently than you might. (This might include vocabulary, grammar, syntax, punctuation, etc.)

Include setting (and sense of place), activity, objects.

300 words.

PART TWO

Now, without referring to the scene you've just written, write this same scene, from the same person's perspective, this time using **Third-Person point of view**. (Compare the salient pages in "When the Narrator is Close.")

Do not change to the point of view of the other character.

The point of the exercise is to explore the SAME character, from First, and then Third person perspectives.

This is not as simple as changing the pronoun "I" to "she" or "he."

For instance: The scene is about Mark trying to tell Jenny that he loves her. Part One is written from Mark's First Person perspective. Part Two is Mark's Third Person perspective. Do not switch to Jenny's point of view.

While there is no expectation that you replicate the first-person scene, the characters and the conflict/tension should remain the same.

Write Part Two without referring to Part One. Watch what happens to the details you choose in first and then in third, and how you utilize them. Perhaps the scene may begin or end in a different place, or the tension may manifest in different ways.

Explore the ways in which language, voice, the sense of distance or involvement, even action and dialogue, change when you move from first person to third.

Reveal, through careful selection of detail, the character doing the perceiving. Once in first person, and then—the same narrator—in Third.

This may include:

What your narrator chooses to observe (sensory perception & proximity)

How s/he describes what's observed.

Language: vocabulary, sentence length, syntax, grammar, colloquial language, figures of speech.

300 words.

16

THROUGH OPPOSITE EYES
OR
THE OTHER SIDE OF THE PICTURE

Inhabit the point of view of the **other person,** that is, **the other side** of the conflict you explored in a previous exercise, such as "Tell Me, then Show Me," or "Through Close Eyes."

Be sure your objectives, the wants of your characters, are clear—they may change when you inhabit this other perspective. Ditto the obstacles. (See "Setting up a Scene.")

Inhabit this point of view as thoroughly as you did the other side of the conflict. Make his/her observations and reflections, however "foreign" to you, as sympathetic, as realized, as grounded as you can.

Choose the voice consciously, with a <u>purpose</u>— using First or Third. If someone were to ask you why you chose First instead of Third might you be able to "defend" the selection? You might try the exercise using both possibilities, and see what you discover.

I suggest that you write this scene without much reference to the previous one. While you want to keep the tension somewhat the same, do not limit yourself to the "reality" established in the previous exercise. This character will probably see his or her needs quite differently; the objectives and the obstacles may be very different when explored from this new perspective. (This is a useful exercise to explore when you are stuck on a scene or you feel that you haven't yet developed a particular character.)

An extra emphasis: Choose to make the vocabulary and syntax of one character be slightly or thoroughly different than those of the other.

→ If different dialogue or phrasing emerges, explore it.

→ Explore sentence length, vocabulary, grammar: manifest the persona.

→ Ditto with the details this character observes.

→ Continue to work on showing rather than telling the tension in the scene.

→ Continue to work on sense of place, activity, objects.

→ Concentrate on SOP: what this character observes: what and how things are observed that will communicate the character to the reader.

300 words.

17

THROUGH EYES THAT SLIDE

Select a scene you have already written, or create a new one that contains three or more characters. (See "Setting up a Scene.") Employing two or three of those characters, try sliding the perspective from narrator to narrator.

If Anne Tyler were to try this exercise with the beginning of her novel, *Ladder of Years* (see the excerpt in "In Things," page 82), she might start the point of view with a young man unloading produce in the produce section of the supermarket. This young man observes Delia enter the store, and also takes in the well-dressed man near the onions; the perspective might then slide to that man—who watches his "ex-wife up ahead in potatoes," and then, as he takes in Delia, the point of view slides to her, as she "languidly" begins to choose her bunch of celery.

Be conscious of your transitions: how you move from far to near, or from one character's "head" to another's. (See "Moving the Point of View.") Make these as smooth as possible; try not to "jar" the reader.

Keep in mind how sensory perceptions can assist you in creating, maintaining, or changing proximity and distance.

350 - 500 words.

18

SOME RAINY DAY

Some rainy day, or on a day when you have a little time and feel like musing, sit next to the bookshelves where you keep your fiction, and pull out one of your novels. Take a look at page one and determine who is telling the story. Is it narrated in First Person? Third? Is an omniscient narrator telling the story? If it's the latter, read on a bit and see if and when the omniscient lands in a particular point of view, and note how the writer accomplishes it.

Then leaf ahead a few chapters and read again. Is the story still being told from the same point of view? If not, who is narrating the story now? When and how did it change?

If the same character is telling the story throughout the pages of this novel, note a few characteristics of the narration—vocabulary, sentence structure, issues of voice, that sort of thing. Then put that novel aside and pick up another.

If the narrator has changed, leaf through the pages to discover a bit more about that. Is the author sliding the narration somewhere, and can you note when and how that happens? Is the author rotating narrators at section or chapter breaks? How many narrators are there? Do they rotate in first person? Do they rotate in third? Does the author use first and third to tell her story—and if so, can you remember, from reading the novel, what purpose the author might have had to choose that technique?

If the novel remains omniscient, note that, and again see how and where the omniscience may slide into a closer perspective.

Dip into the novel in this way several times, until you feel that you have a good sense, in a somewhat superficial way (that is, without reading or rereading the novel) of what the author is doing. Then put the book back and do the same with another book.

You can also do this with a volume of short stories. The point is to ascertain, quickly and easily, how a writer is working with point of view, and perhaps to take some of what you discover back to your own writing.

19

THROUGH DISTANT EYES

Select a scene: one developed from an exercise in this volume, from something you're currently writing, or something you are interested in writing. Applying the attributes for a distant narrator described in "When a Narrator has Distance," try writing (or rewriting) a scene incorporating that point of view.

Keep in mind how a distant narrator might be different from an omniscient one (that is, not rising out to a larger perspective; save that for your explorations with omniscience).

For instance, you might keep to the perspective of a particular character, relating what he or she knows, but also utilize the strengths of this perspective, which is an ability to pull out and look at and—physically, emotionally and psychologically—describe him or her.

Make it part of your effort not to move too thoroughly or quickly into your narrator's thoughts.

When you do, give us only what that narrator is thinking, without (for the purposes of this exercise) moving into the point of view of other characters.

Another option is to present a character distant from himself, and use that sense of distance in the point of view to let the reader understand that about the character.

Keep in mind how sensory perceptions can assist you in creating, maintaining, or changing proximity and distance.

250 - 400 words.

20

THROUGH OMNISCIENT EYES

Select a scene—one you've written or want to write—in which it is useful to employ the large eye of omniscience.

Keep in mind the derivations of the word: all-knowing.

What makes an omniscient narrator different from third person?

Use the image of a swooping camera that can start anywhere and go anywhere, and explore the possibilities this offers you. (See "Moving the Point of View.")

What kinds of details—scenic, historical, emotional—might you be able to include that, for instance, no single character in the scene might know?

You may find yourself starting a scene earlier than you might otherwise, establishing history or geography or psychology—or providing details only an omniscient narrator would know about the lives and even futures of your characters.

Keep in mind how sensory perceptions can assist you in creating, maintaining, or changing proximity and distance.

Among the things you might play with and try to incorporate:

(a)   A voice with authority, or with an attitude.

(b)   A wide lens on the scene: geographical, historical, psychological

(c)   Pulling close to a particular character or characters

(d)   Looking at your characters from outside, giving an opinion about them

(e)   Moving in to occupy one or the other of their points of view

(f)   A slide or shift to another character,

and/or

(g)   back out to the larger perspective.

500 - 1000 words.

21

POINT OF VIEW, DIALOGUE, & SENSE OF PLACE

Continue to work with characters and a setting established in a previous exercise, such as "Through Close Eyes" or "Through Opposite Eyes"; or choose one of the narrators you may have come to know in writing "My Two Grandmothers" or "Through Other Eyes"; or select a scene you want to work on from a manuscript in progress. For the purposes of this scene, there should be a specific, probably close (first or third) point of view you intend to explore.

Once you are sure of the point of view (who will narrate the scene), establish setting and activity and character objectives. If you have not done so already, try jotting down what you want the scene to accomplish.

Character A is in or enters a place. Character B is there, or enters, wanting something specific from A.

Keeping in mind the various dialogue pitfalls, and maintaining a sense of the setting as well as of the other character(s), write a scene in which A or B's objectives do or do not get accomplished.

While your dialogue should reflect the objectives as well as the nature of each of your characters (utilizing, for example, sentence structure, vocabulary, grammar), the focus here is on including and maintaining the point of view through the sense of place. Reveal things about your narrator through not only <u>what</u> they observe but <u>how</u> they report that to the reader.

How does the point of view reveal aspects of her nature as well as her emotions and opinions to the reader? This does not mean using inner thought about what she is feeling, but conveying this information through her perceptions of what and who is in the space with her.

As a way to remind yourself to incorporate these notions, include references to your setting (at least two), several moments in which we see a physical aspect of at least one of your characters, and at least three actions/gestures/movements. Each of these should reveal something about how your narrator is viewing the unfolding situation and/or the other character(s) in the scene.

300 words.

22

THREE LINES OF DIALOGUE

Reveal Character A in a place (setting), doing something (activity). Character B might already be in the scene, or B might enter. Either way, B, who has an ISSUE s/he wants to address, interrupts or ignores or engages or irritates A (A also has an objective—something s/he is trying to get done). Make sure you know where the point of view is.

You get to employ three lines of dialogue.

All the dialogue can be spoken by one person. Or each of your characters gets at least one line. A line is defined by anything that ends in a full stop: a period; it can be one word or a punctuation-free monologue.

At no point is the conflict directly addressed by the dialogue.

Continue to use setting and gesture and action, not necessarily something your characters say, to communicate information to the reader. And again, avoid inner thought as a way of revealing the scene's "real" content to your reader.

150 - 250 words.

23

DIALOGUE: EMPLOYING SYNTAX AND VOCABULARY

Feel free to continue or experiment with the characters and setting and point of view you established in any of the previous exercises. If it will serve you better, start anew.

Again, make sure you establish setting and activity and character objectives. Before you begin, you might try jotting down what you want the scene to accomplish.

The focus here is to use sentence structure and sentence length, grammar, vocabulary, including colloquialisms or figures of speech, to create different voices for your characters as they speak.

Again: we find Character A in a place, doing something. Character B is there, or enters, wanting something specific from A.

Play with the idea that Character A uses with one kind of speech pattern, Character B another. Use these to underscore differences between your characters.

In other words, experiment with people who speak differently—from the way YOU speak (and think) and from the way your other characters speak (and think).

150 - 250 words.

24

DIALOGUE: SOME SPECIAL CASES

PART ONE: A MONOLOGUING CHARACTER

Put a character in a setting, with an activity (again, you can use something already established or start anew), and give him a monologue that reveals something about him and something he wants.

Use syntax and grammar and vocabulary to let us understand who this character is and why s/he is going on at great length in this way.

Keep the "camera" active —now and again draw the reader's eye to setting and activity, etc. Make sure each of those choices reveals something.

PART TWO: ON THE PHONE

Establish setting, activity and put a character on the phone. (Think of all we do while we're talking on the phone).

Depending on the point of view, you can let us hear one or both sides of the conversation. Let the stakes be high. Reveal what the stakes are—the objective is—only through action and dialogue (but not exposition-y dialogue!)

Again, keep the "camera" active; use the setting and activity within and around the dialogue.

PART THREE: NO TAGS

Try a brief exchange of dialogue in which you make it clear who is speaking not by action but by what each character says.

Briefly establish setting and activity, but differentiate the characters—and keep characters' objectives clear — not in what they do but through what they say.

Still, keep the tension between the lines, not <u>on</u> the lines! Maintain character and conflict through dialogue ONLY.

PART FOUR: DIALECT

Perhaps you have a character that hails from a different region or country.

You can give him a monologue, above, or you can put him in a scene—establishing why he s there and what he wants.

Let us "hear" this character, without necessarily re-spelling the words he speaks. Instead, use rhythm and sentence structure to give us a sense of the character's voice.

Don't forget to let us see him/her and setting/ activity as well.

Each: 75 - 100 words.

25

WHAT DOES THIS SCENE NEED TO ACCOMPLISH?

Write a sentence or paragraph, or just jot some notes, that describe what you think a scene needs to accomplish. In these notes, describe what it is you intend to move forward in your story by writing this scene.

Some checkpoints:

→ Have your objective as author in place: why the scene needs to take place.

→ Also: What each character wants, what's in the way of their getting what they want, where the scene is set and activities in which the characters might be involved.

Further questions to ponder:

→ What happens by the end of the scene?

→ Does someone get what s/he wants?

→ Do they not?

→ Do they still want it? Do they want something else?

→ Does the end of this scene launch some subsequent scenes? How?

Some Dialogue questions:

→   How do the natures of these characters
     emerge when they talk?

→   That is, though their vocabulary, grammar,
     sentence length, syntax

→   How, besides words, might they communi-
     cate? As ways to establish and/or maintain
     character, might they incorporate:

     ■ Silence
     ■ Excess verbiage
     ■ Gesture and action versus speech

→   Also: Can you activate, during the scene, the
     setting and activity you've selected to reveal
     something about your characters and charac-
     ter objectives?

Sense of place: can you maintain and strengthen the
point of view by what and how your character perceives?

If they occur to you, jot down other levels or metaphors you might want to incorporate or communicate.

JOT DOWN AS MUCH
AS YOU NEED TO GET STARTED
(this will vary, writer to writer and scene to scene),

THEN PUT YOUR CHARACTERS INTO ACTION.

BIBLIOGRAPHY
OF QUOTED AND CITED SOURCES

Akutagawa, Ryunosuke. *Rashomon and Other Stories*. New York: Liveright, 1952.

Atwood, Margaret. *The Blind Assassin*. New York : N.A. Talese, 2000.

— "You Fit Into Me", in *Anthology of Modern Poetry*, 2nd ed. New York: W.W. Norton & Co., 1988.

— *The Robber Bride*. New York: Nan A. Talese/Doubleday, 1993.

Austen, Jane. *Pride and Prejudice*. New York: Knopf, 1991.

— *Sense and Sensibility*. New York: Dutton, 1973.

Bambara, Toni Cade. "The Lesson", in *Gorilla My Love*. New York: Random House, 1972.

Byrd, Max. *Grant*. New York: Bantam Books, 2000.

Carver, Raymond. "Cathedral", in *Cathedral: Stories*. New York: Vintage Books, 1989.

Childress, Mark. *Crazy in Alabama*. New York: Putnam, 1993.

Connell, Evan S. *Mrs. Bridge*. San Francisco: North Point, 1981.

Conroy, Pat. *Beach Music*. New York: N.A. Talese, 1995.

Cooper, Stephen. "The Paper Man," in *The Critic*. Spring 1990 vol. 44, No. 3.

Crane, Stephen. "The Bride Comes to Yellow Sky", in *Short Story Masterpieces*. New York: Dell, 1982.

Cunningham, Michael. *The Hours*. New York: Farrar, Straus, Giroux, 1998.

Dillard, Annie. "Living like Weasels", in *The Annie Dillard Reader*. New York: HarperPerennial, 1995.

Egan, Jennifer. "Emerald City", in *Emerald City and Other Stories*. New York: N.A. Talese, 1996.

— *The Invisible Circus*. New York: Nan A. Talese/Doubleday, 1989.

— *Look at Me*. New York: Nan A. Talese/Doubleday, 2001.

Faulkner, William. "A Rose for Emily", in M. Cowley, ed., *The Portable Faulkner*. New York: Viking press, 1946.

— *The Sound and the Fury*. New York: Vintage Books, 1990.

Faulks, Sebastian. *Birdsong*. New York: Random House, 1996.

Foote, Mary Hallock. *A Victorian Gentlewoman in the Far West: The Reminiscences of Mary Hallock Foote*. Paul W. Rodman, ed. San Marino, CA: Huntington Library, 1972.

Fowler, Karen Joy. *The Jane Austen Book Club*. New York: Putnam, 2004.

Fowles, John. *The French Lieutenant's Woman*. Boston: Little, Brown and Company, 1969.

Frazier, Charles. *Cold Mountain*. New York: Atlantic Monthly Press, 1997.

Frost, Robert. "Mending Wall", in Gary D. Schmidt, ed., *Robert Frost: Poetry for Young People*. New York: Sterling Publishing Co., 1994.

— Frost, Robert. "The Road Not Taken", in *The Road Not Taken: a Selection Of Robert Frost's* Poems. New York: H. Holt, 1985.

Gardner, John. *The Art of Fiction*. New York: A. Knopf, 1983.

— *On Moral Fiction*. New York: Basic Books, 1978.

Glass, Julia. *Three Junes*. New York: Pantheon Books, 2002.

Goldberg, Myla. *Bee Season*. New York: Doubleday, 2000.

Guterson, David. *Snow Falling on Cedars*. New York: Harcourt Brace, 1994.

Hall, Oakley. *Warlock*. Reno: University of Nevada Press, 1986.

— *Separations*. Reno: University of Nevada Press, 1997.

Hall, Sands. *Catching Heaven*. New York: Ballantine, 2000.

Hamilton, Jane. *A Map of the World*. New York: Doubleday, 1994.

Heaney, Seamus. "Digging", in *Death of a Naturalist and Other Poems*. New York: Oxford University Press, 1966.

Hemingway, Ernest. "Hills Like White Elephants", in *Hemingway, The Short Stories*. New York: Scribner Classics, 1997.

Huffy, Rhoda. *The Hallelujah Side*. Harrison, New York: Delphinium Books, 1999.

Hughes, Langston. "Harlem", in *Selected Poems of Langston Hughes*. New York: Vintage Books, 1990.

Ibsen, Henrik. "Peer Gynt", in *Ibsen's Selected Plays*. New York: W.W. Norton, 2004.

Ishiguro, Kazuo. *Remains of the Day*. New York: A.A. Knopf, 1989.

Jackson, Shirley. *We Have Always Lived in the Castle*. New York: Viking, 1962.

James, Henry. *The Portrait of a Lady*. New York: Modern Library, 1983.

Johnson, Diane. *Le Divorce*. New York: Dutton, 1997.

Jones, Louis B. *California's Over*. New York: Pantheon Books, 1997.

Kingsolver, Barbara. *The Poisonwood Bible*. New York: HarperFlamingo, 1998.

McInerney, Jay. *Bright Lights, Big City*. New York: Vintage Contemporaries, 1984.

McMurtry, Larry. *Lonesome Dove*. New York: Simon and Schuster, 1985.

Melville, Herman. *Moby Dick*. New York: Vintage Books/Library of America, 1991.

Mitchell, Joni. "Case of You." Lyrics as recorded on *Blue* album, Reprise Records, 1971.

Morrison, Toni. *Beloved*. New York: A.A. Knopf, 1987.

Oates, Joyce Carol. "Where Are You Going, Where Have You Been?" in *Best American Short Stories*. Boston: Houghton-Mifflin, 1967.

Salinger, J. D. *The Catcher in the Rye*. New York: New American Library, 1951.

— "A Perfect Day for Bananafish", in *Nine Stories*. Boston: Little, Brown, 1953.

— "For Esmé with Love and Squalor", in *Nine Stories*. Boston: Little, Brown, 1953.

Sebold, Alice. *The Lovely Bones*. Boston: Little, Brown, 2002.

Simon, Paul. "Graceland." Lyrics as recorded on *Graceland* album, Warner Bros. Records, 1986.

Tan, Amy. "Half & Half", in *The Joy Luck Club*. New York: Putnam, 1989.

Thackeray, William Makepeace. *Vanity Fair*. New York: Knopf, 1991.

Twain, Mark. *The Adventures of Huckleberry Finn*. Philadelphia: Chelsea House Publishers, 2004.

Tyler, Anne. *The Accidental Tourist*. New York: A.A. Knopf, 1985.

— *Ladder of Years*. New York: A.A. Knopf, 1995.

Walker, Alice. *The Color Purple*. New York : Harcourt Brace Jovanovich, 1982.

Webster's New Collegiate Dictionary. Springfield, MA: Merriam-Webster, 2004.

ACKNOWLEDGMENTS

Much of this book came about as a result of my being given opportunities to teach. I want to offer thanks here to some of those who made that possible, above all to Peggy Houston, who founded and for years led the Iowa Summer Writing Festival, as well as the Elderhostel programs on the University of Iowa Campus. Peggy gave me my first job teaching writing and continued to believe in me even after I thought it a good idea to teach Colette's *The Last of Cheri* to an Elderhostel literature class. Blessings on you, Peggy.

Huge bouquets are due her successor, the brilliant Amy Margolis, who inherited a hugely energetic program and who yet finds ways to turn the electricity even higher—what a joy.

I am grateful to Brett Hall Jones, Executive Director of the Community of Writers at Squaw Valley, an organization she leads with a firm, visionary, and always loving hand, as well as to the Community's Director Emeritus, my mentor and friend, Oakley Hall.

Thanks are also due Nancy Kilpatrick, at the University of California, Davis, Extension Programs, for her thoughtfulness, humor, and enthusiasm—and for many good ideas for courses.

To Elizabeth Ann Stewart and Lynne Collins, as well as Dean Frew (who took a chance), at American River College: Thank you for pointing the way towards the teaching of not just writing but literature, an incredibly important step in understanding what authors do to be effective; and for lending me syllabi to pore over and utilize until I began to concoct my own.

Amongst the students who have taught me much are members of the "Gold River Gang," as our beloved and

v

dearly-missed Mary Bolton knew us: Thank you, Francis Sutz Brown, Susan Nicoles, Gary Hart, and Jennie Hansen, as well as Carol Percy and Susan Britton. Thanks also to Nina Krebs, Vonnie Madigan, and Linda Raymond.

Robert Q. Hoyt provided opportunities for passionate and enlightening discussions on point of view—I'm especially grateful for a dissection of Cunningham's *The Hours* undertaken together. And for many a bottle of grand red along the way.

Marjorie Meret deserves a huge thank you for helping to persuade me, long ago, that editing and teaching were something at which I just might be able to make a living, and for the serendipitous times she has needed an editor.

To Debbie Boucher and Margaret de Palma, as well as to Randall Buechner and Romain Nelson (I remember, slightly chagrined-ly, their discussion about who'd heard me go on about Heaney's "Digging" more times), and to many others who go unmentioned here but whose contributions are reflected in these pages: Thank you all for your insights and support.

To the writers about whom I speak and whose work I quote in this book: thank you for the inspiration—to study your work has been, over and over, a reminder and a testament to what I believe good writing is.

And finally: My sublime editor, Steve Susoyev, gave this enormous project his fullest energy—which is saying something—as well as his wisdom and experience as a fellow editor and writer. Even when he had been working for seventeen hours straight, often his e-mails would end, *Whee!* For his enthusiasm, his attention to detail, and his commitment to excellence—and his sense of humor—as well as for myriad contributions, large and small, he has my deepest gratitude.

INDEX